"That love is inexhaustible,
you will be there"
forever

_____

_____

_____

_____

_____

THIS BOOK
Belongs to

_____

_____

Visit Our Author Page At
amazon.com

All rights reserved. No part of this book may be used or reproduced in any manner whatsoever without written permission except in the case of brief quotations embodied in critical articles and interviews.

© by BLACK ROSE PRESS HOUSE

Color This Moon

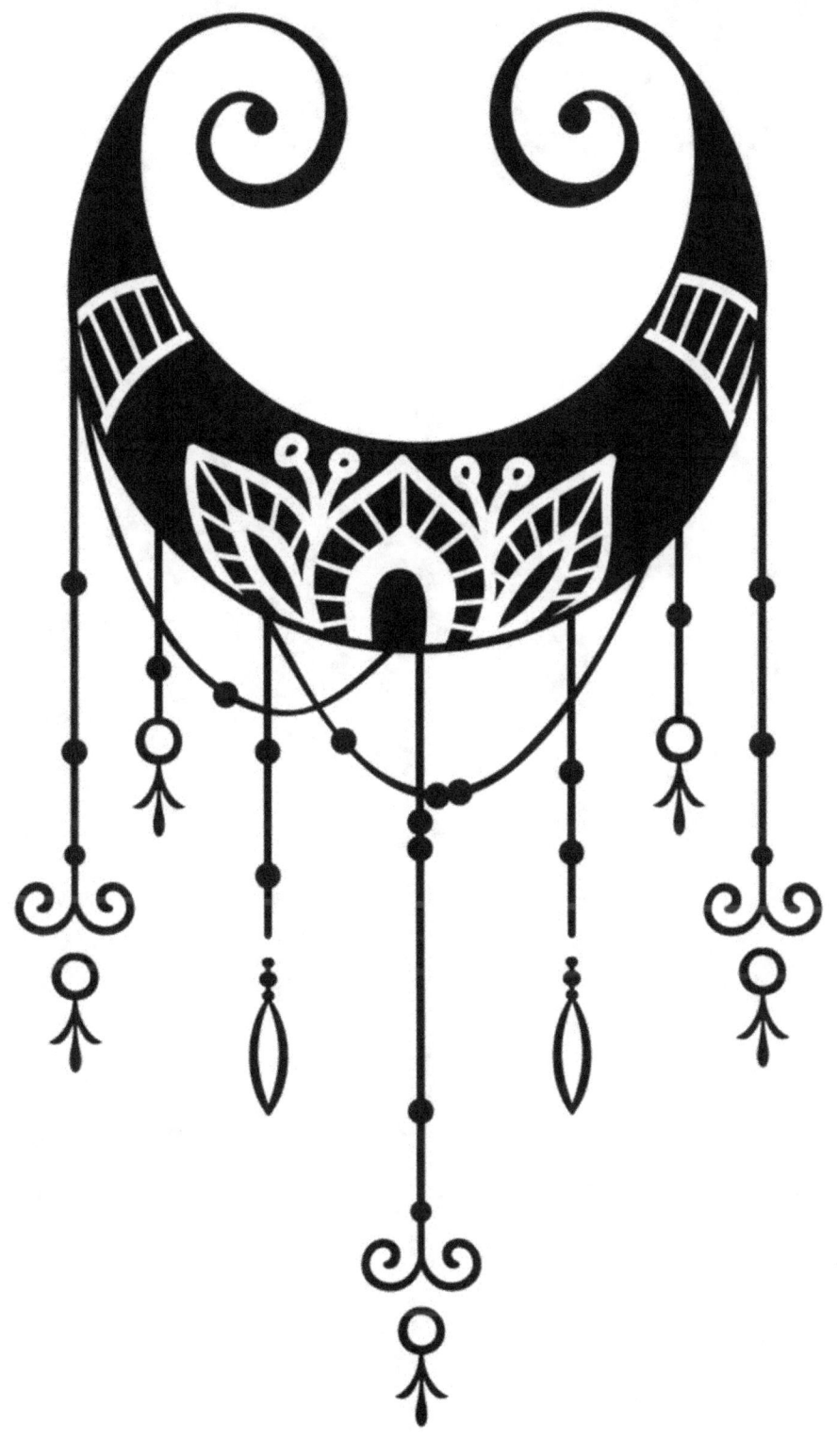

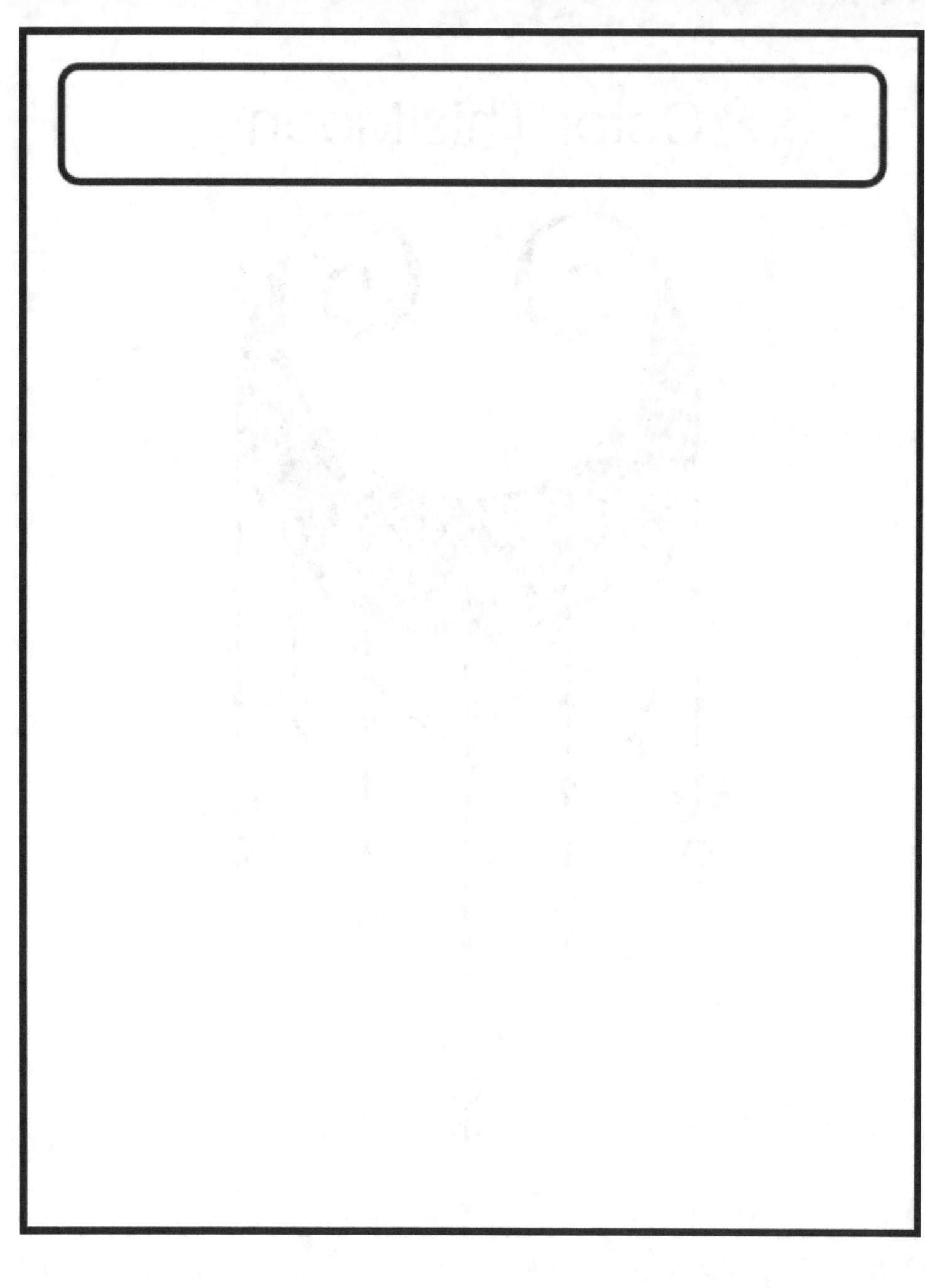

Color This Moon

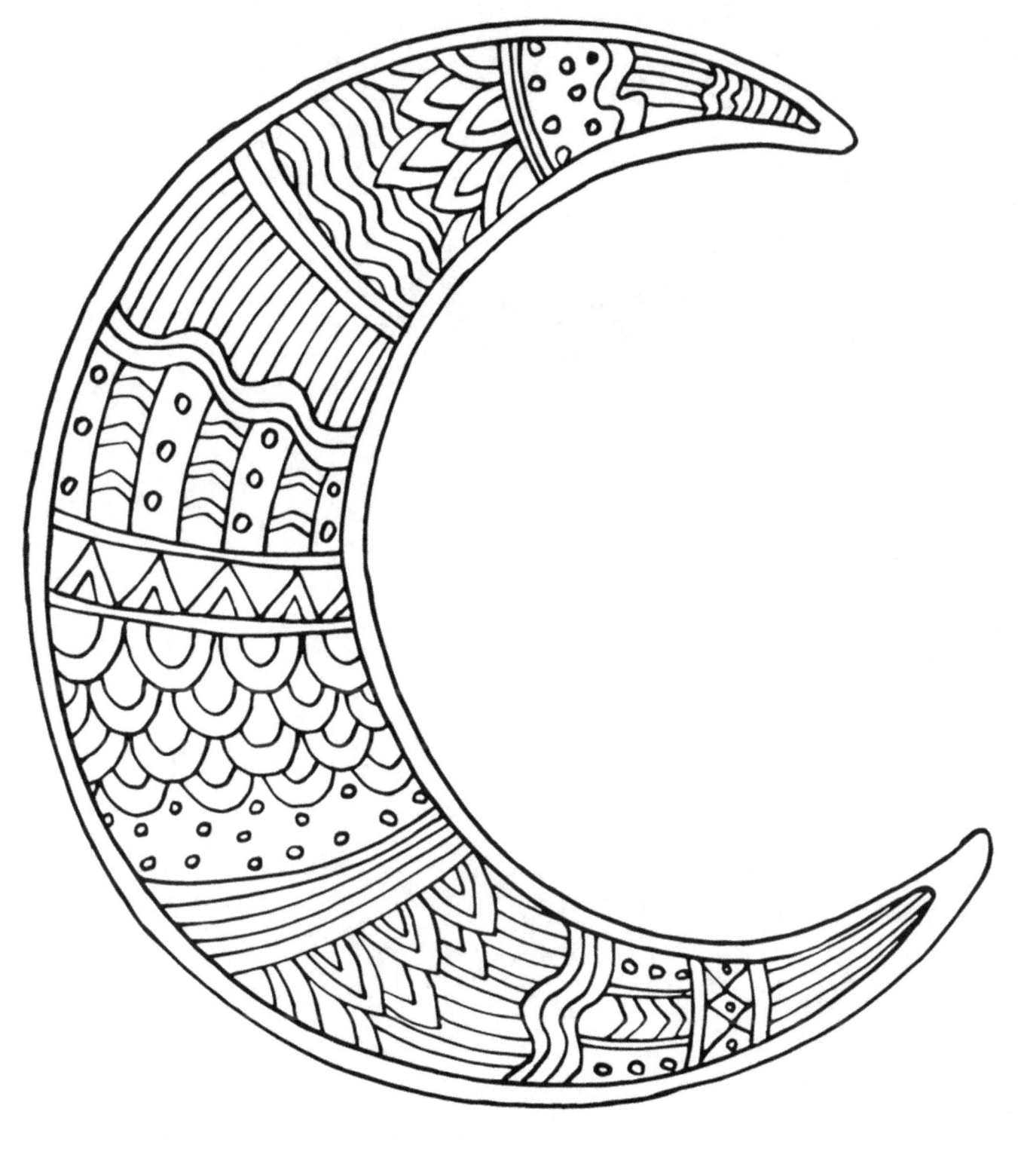

Color This Moon

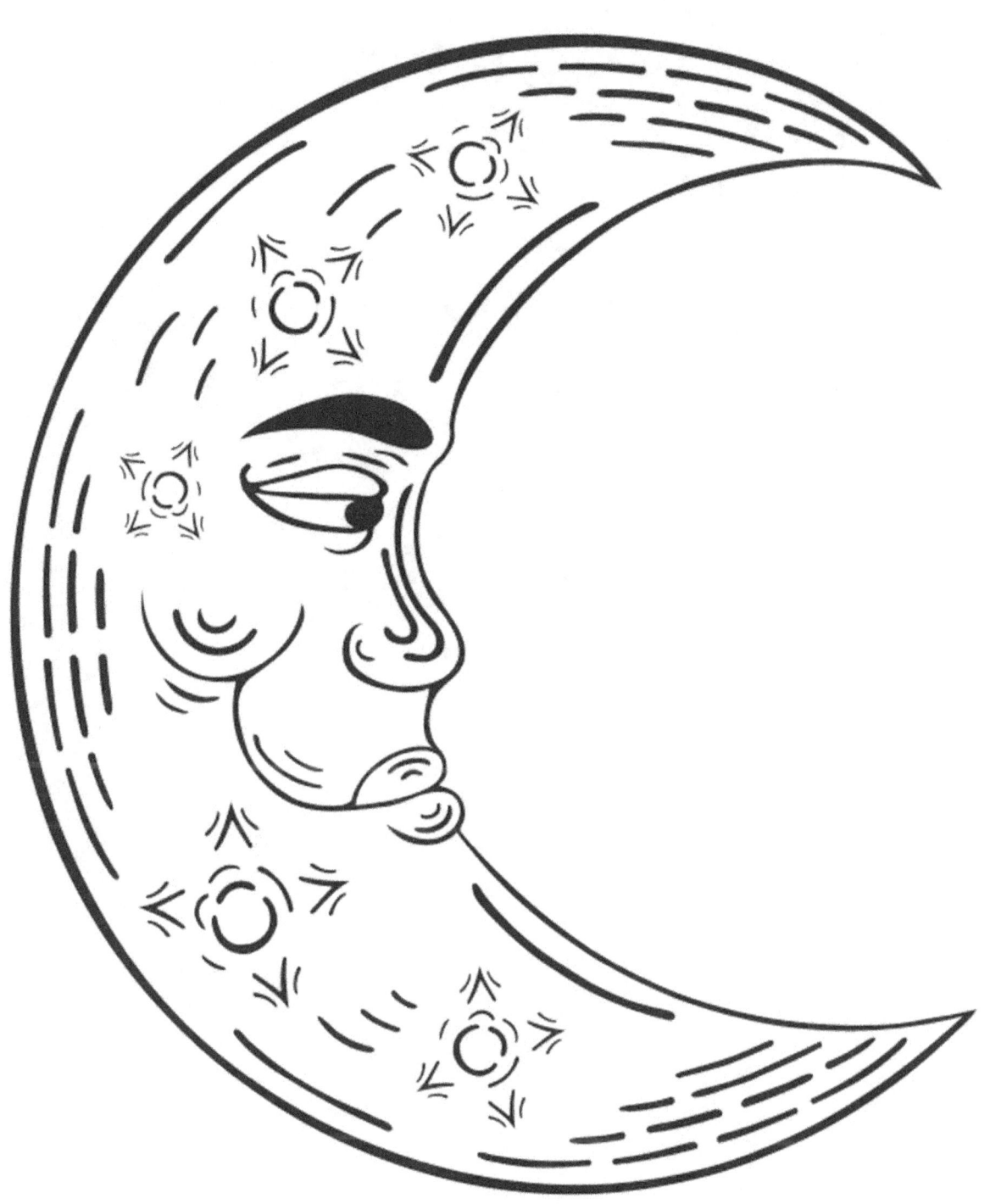

Color This Moon

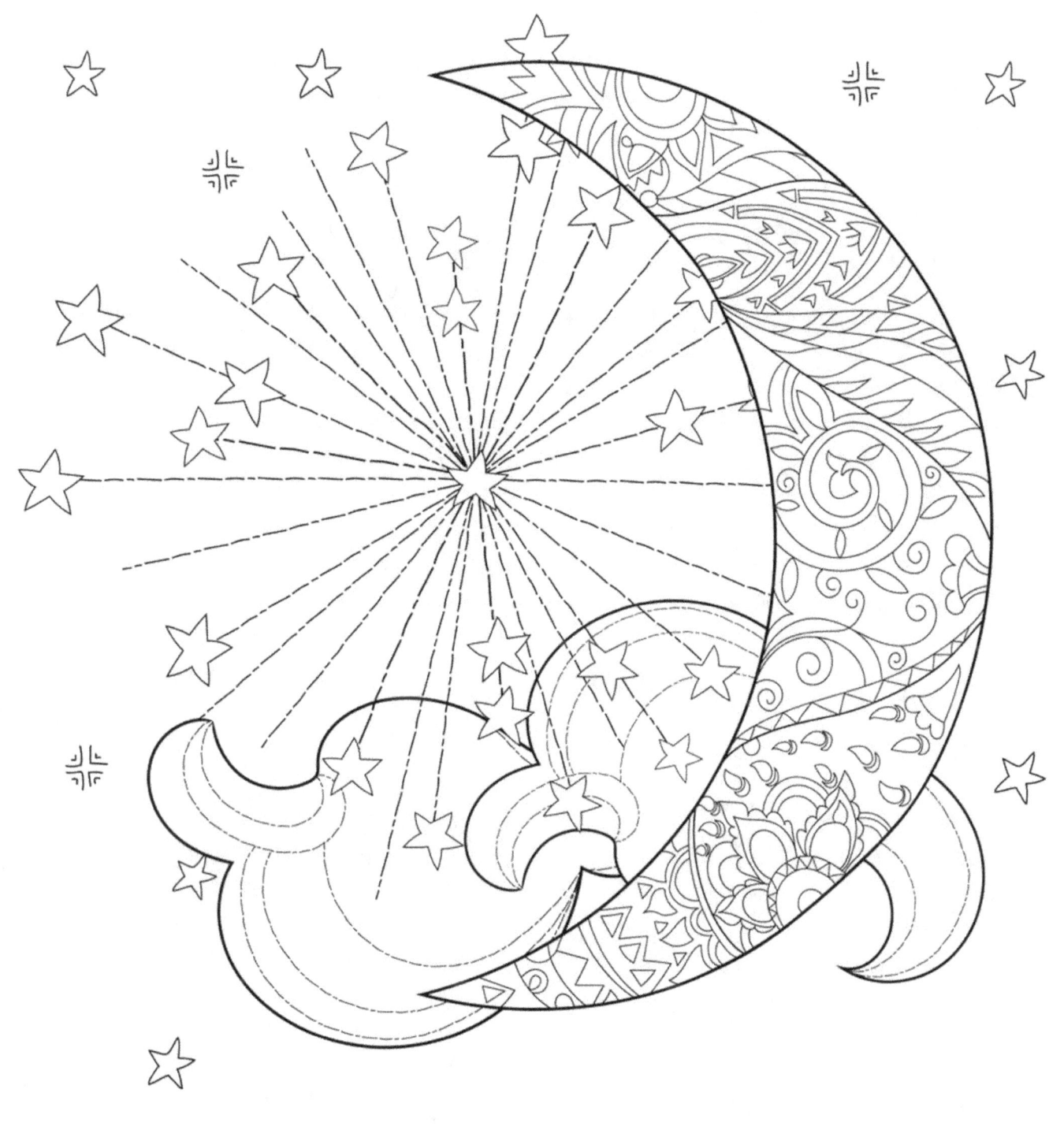

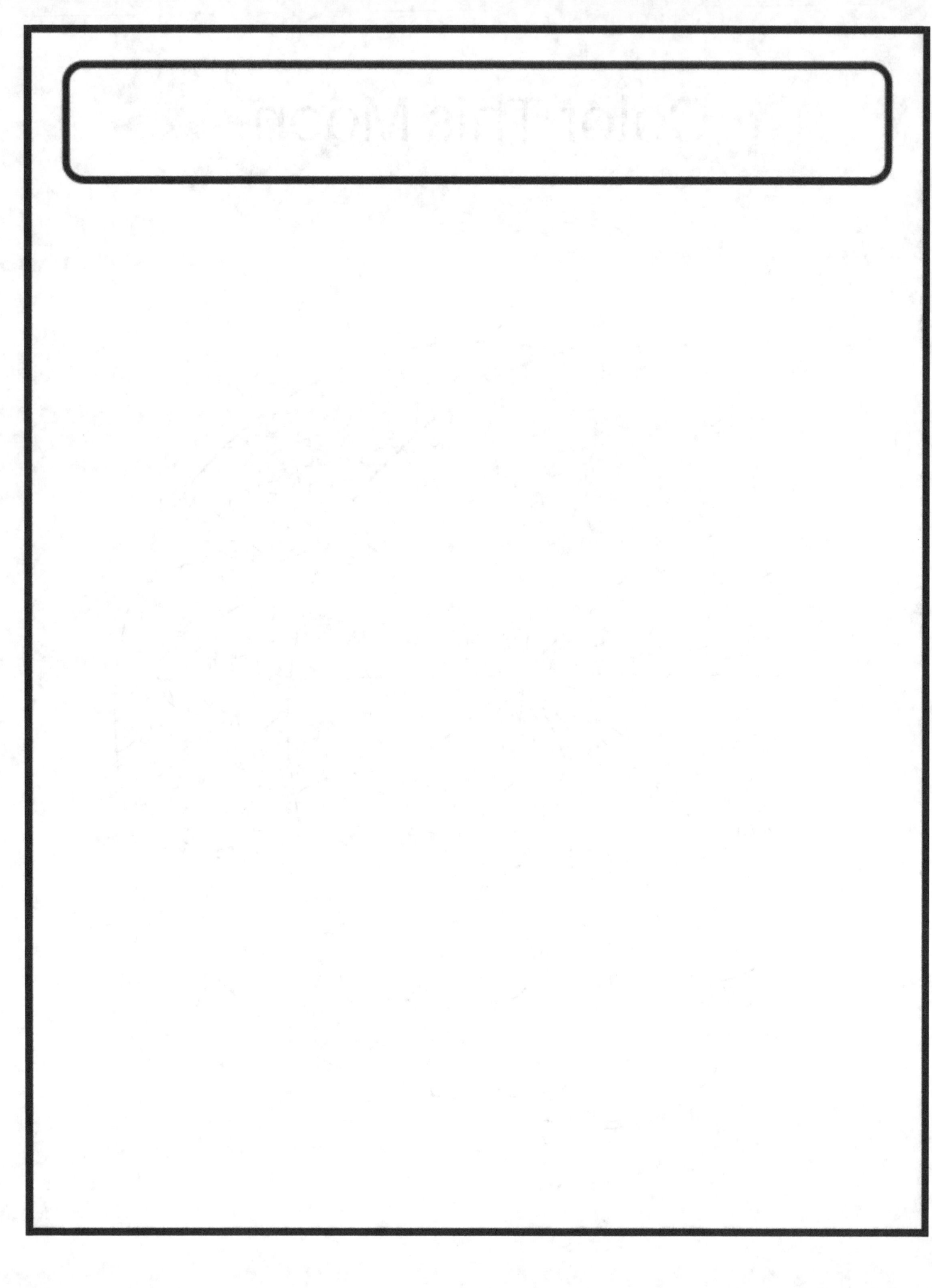

Color This Moon

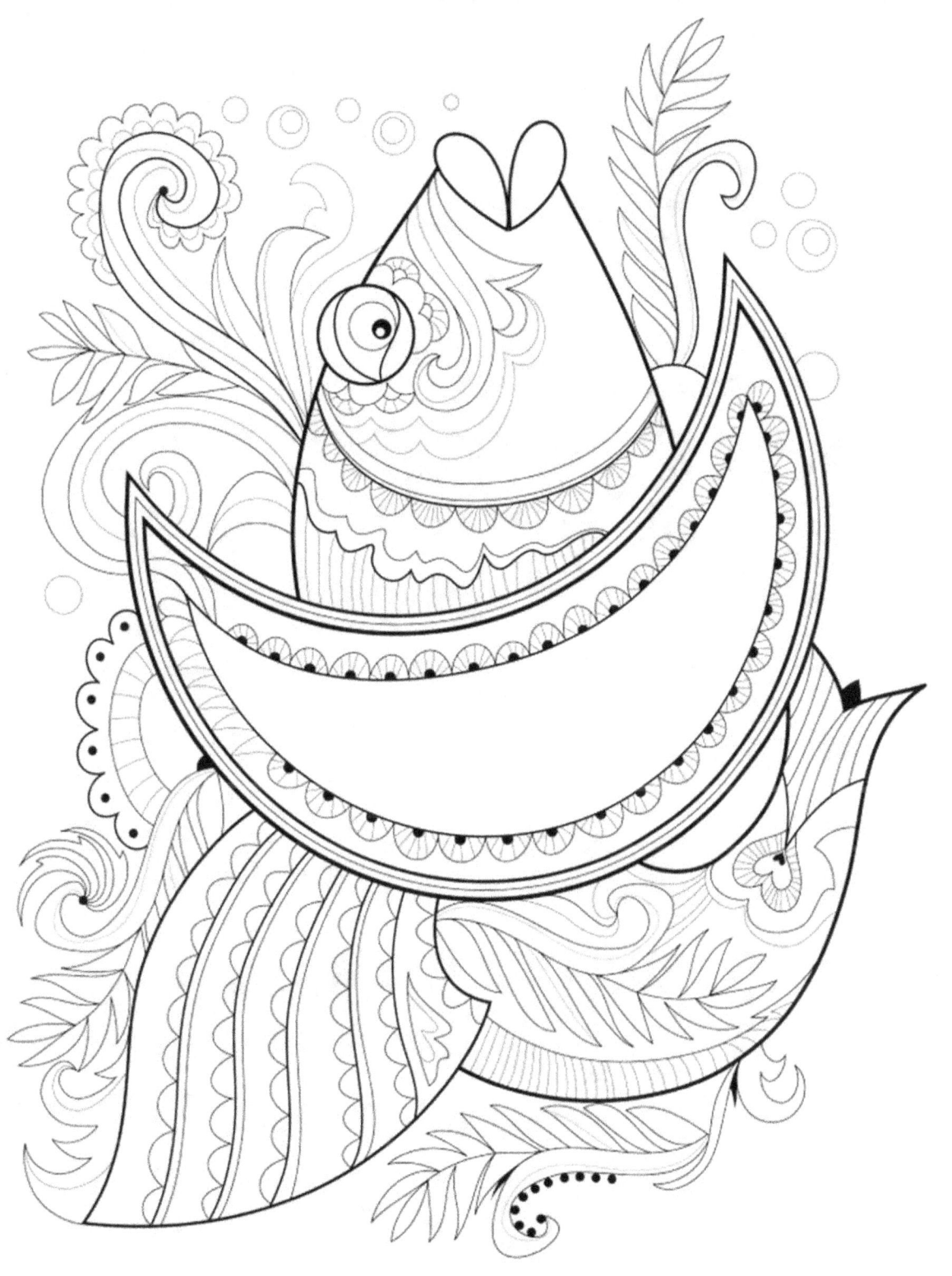

Color This Moon

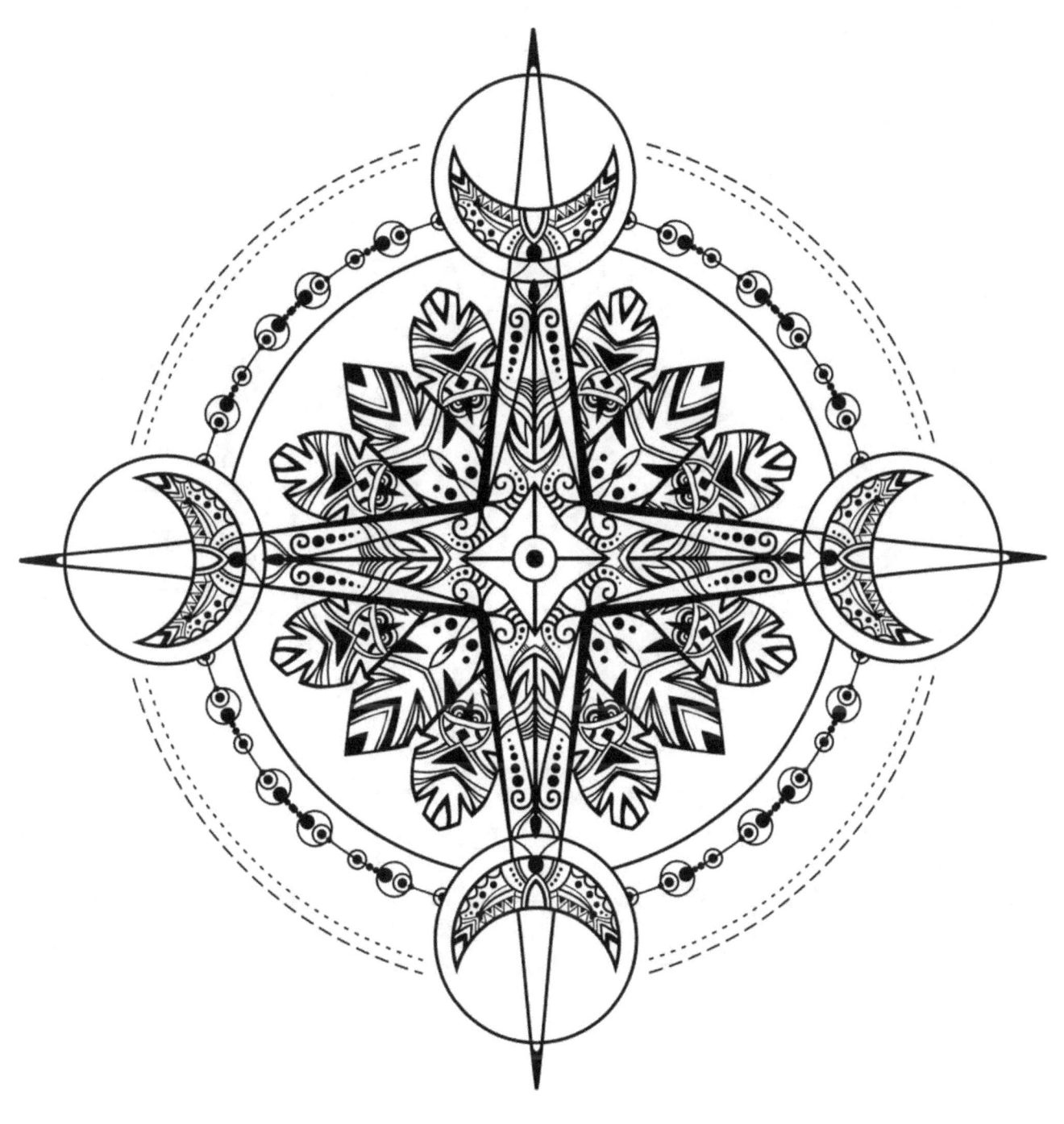

Color This Moon

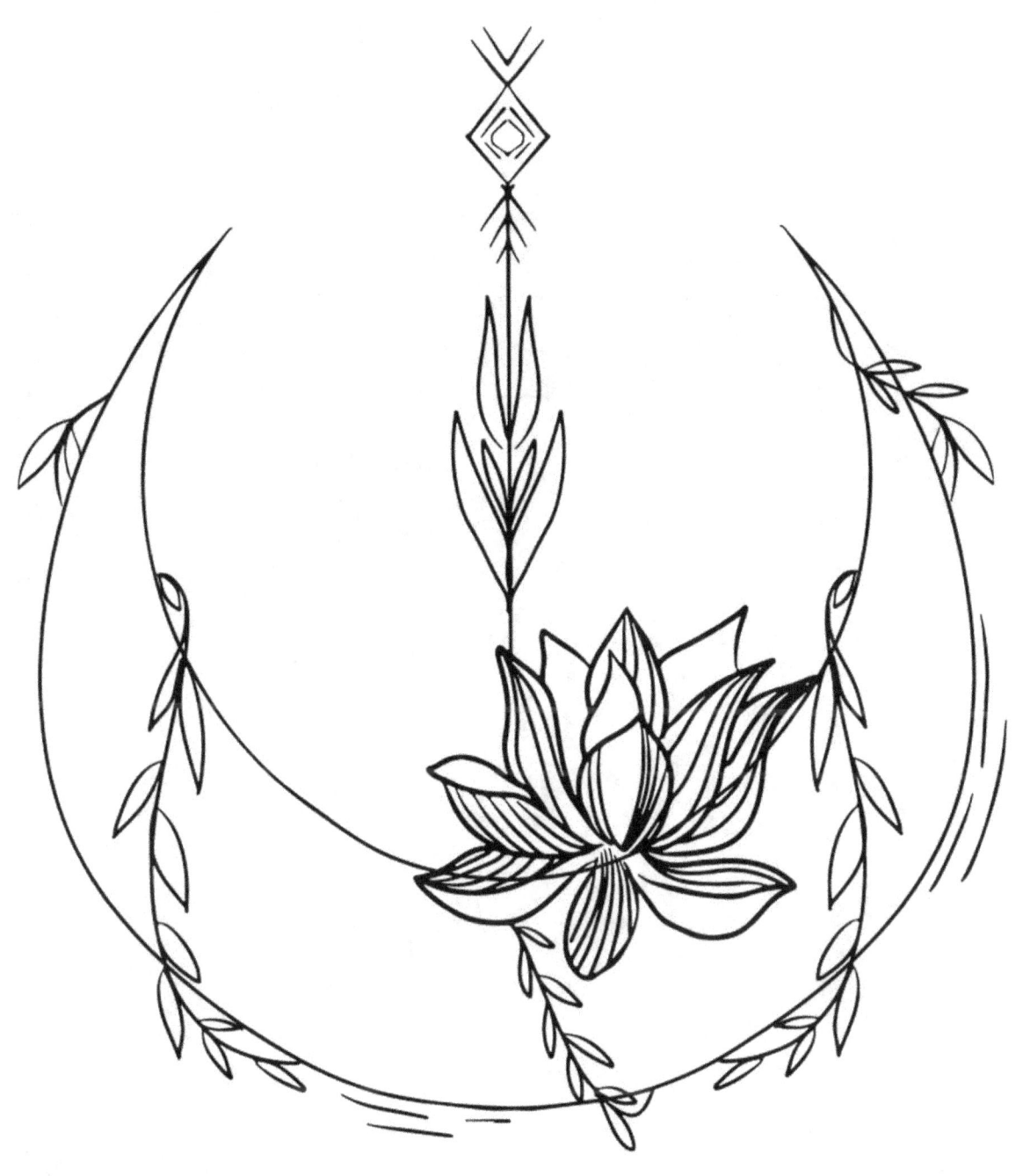

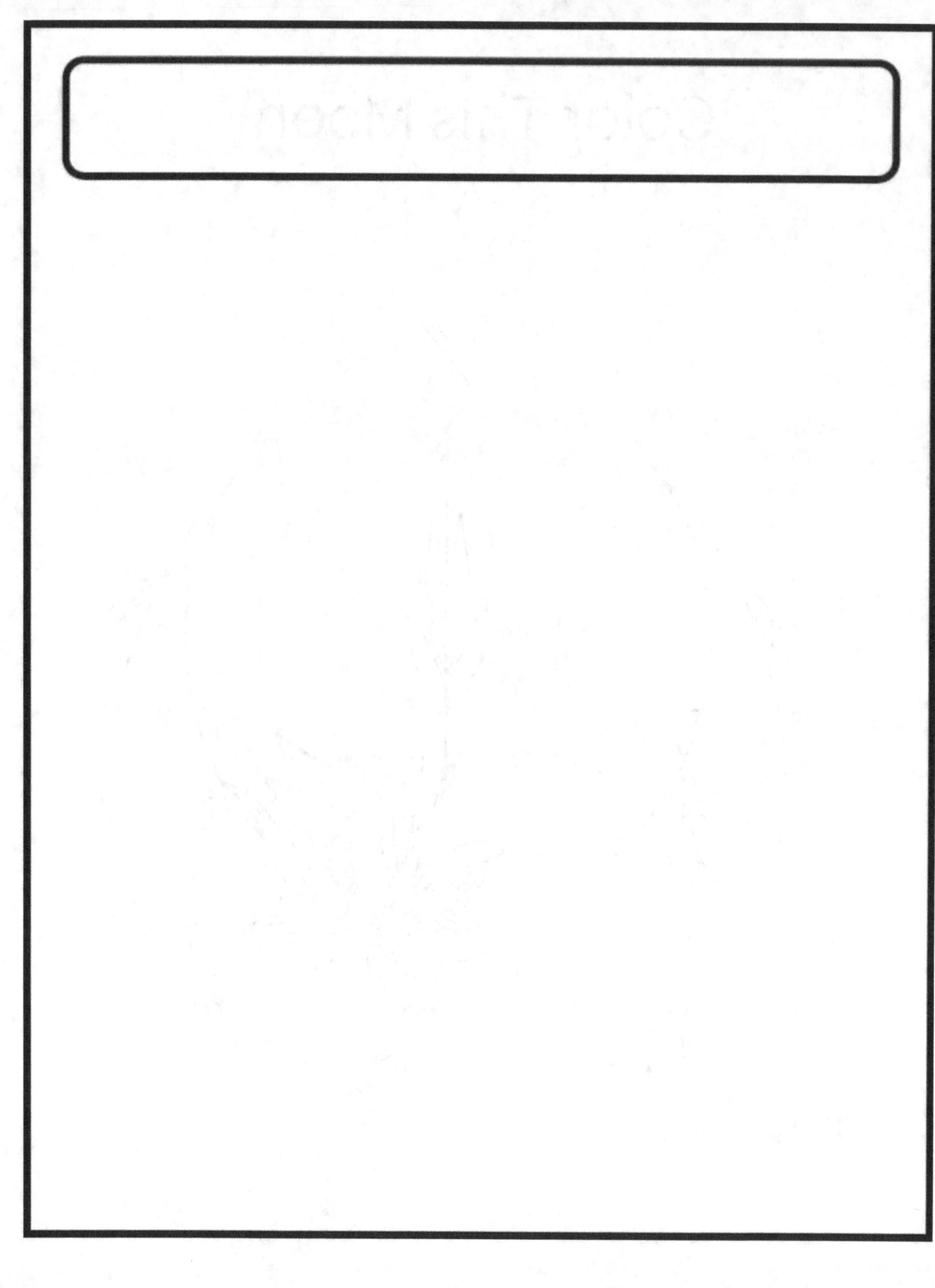

Color This Moon

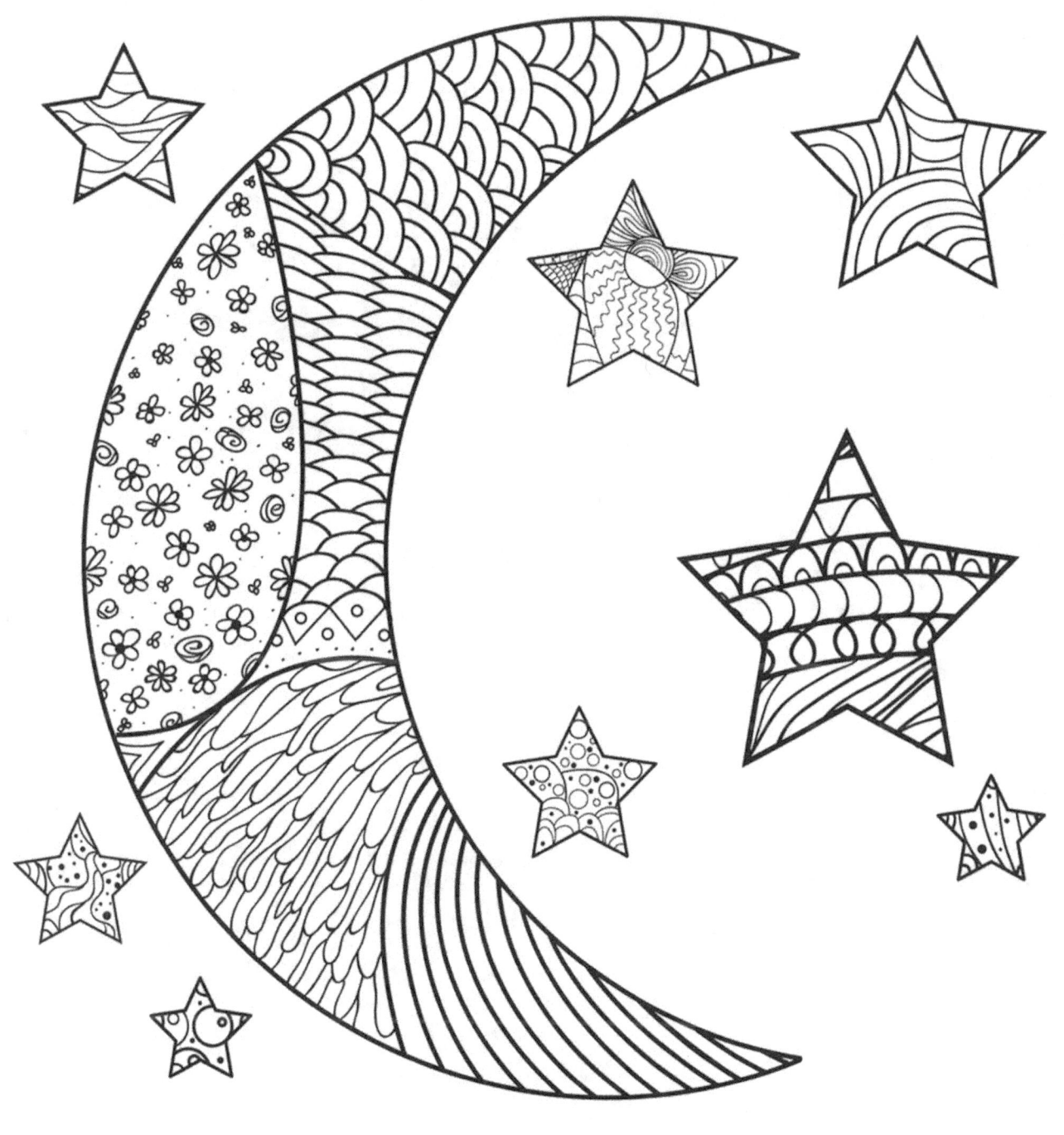

Color This Moon

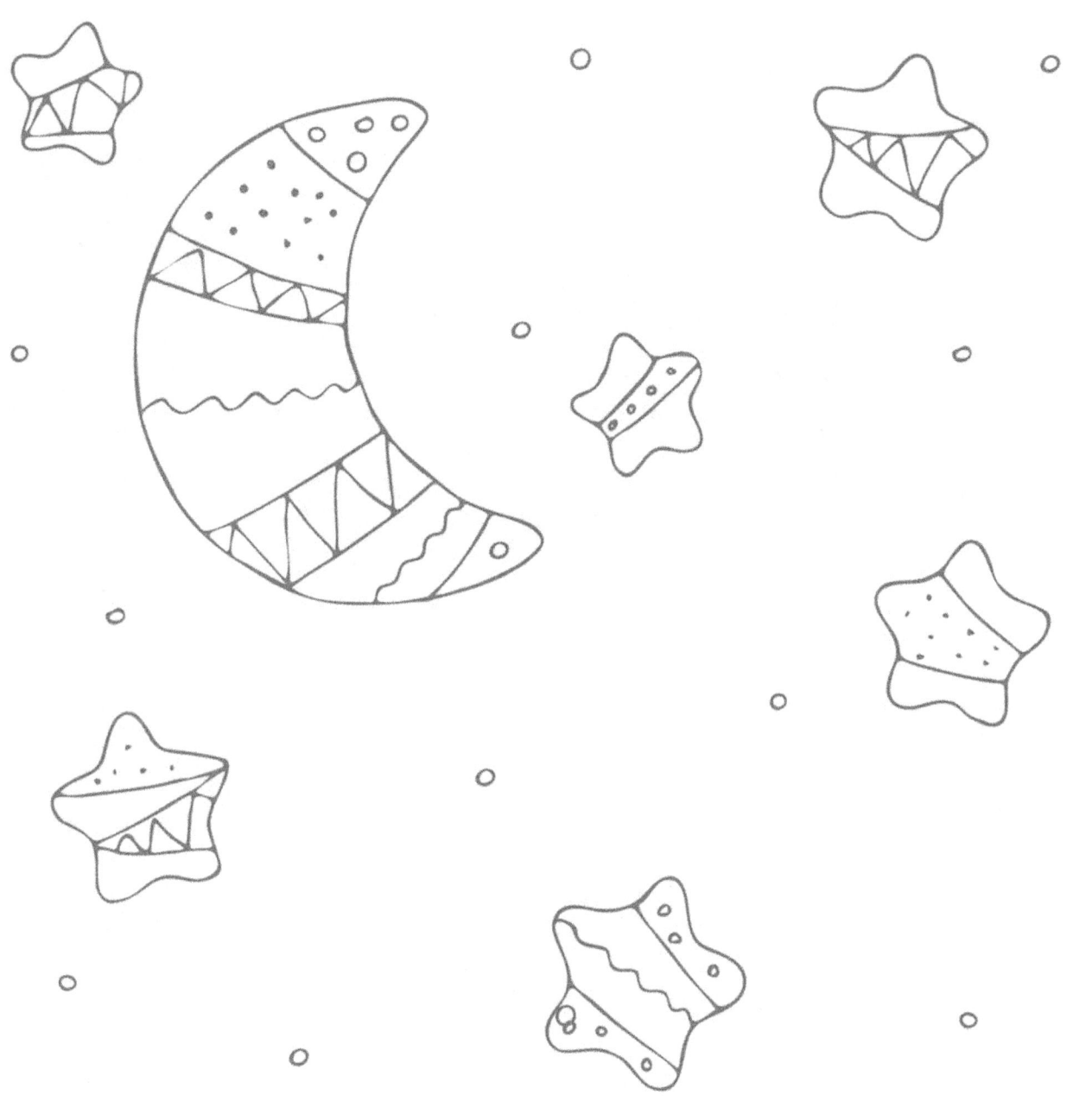

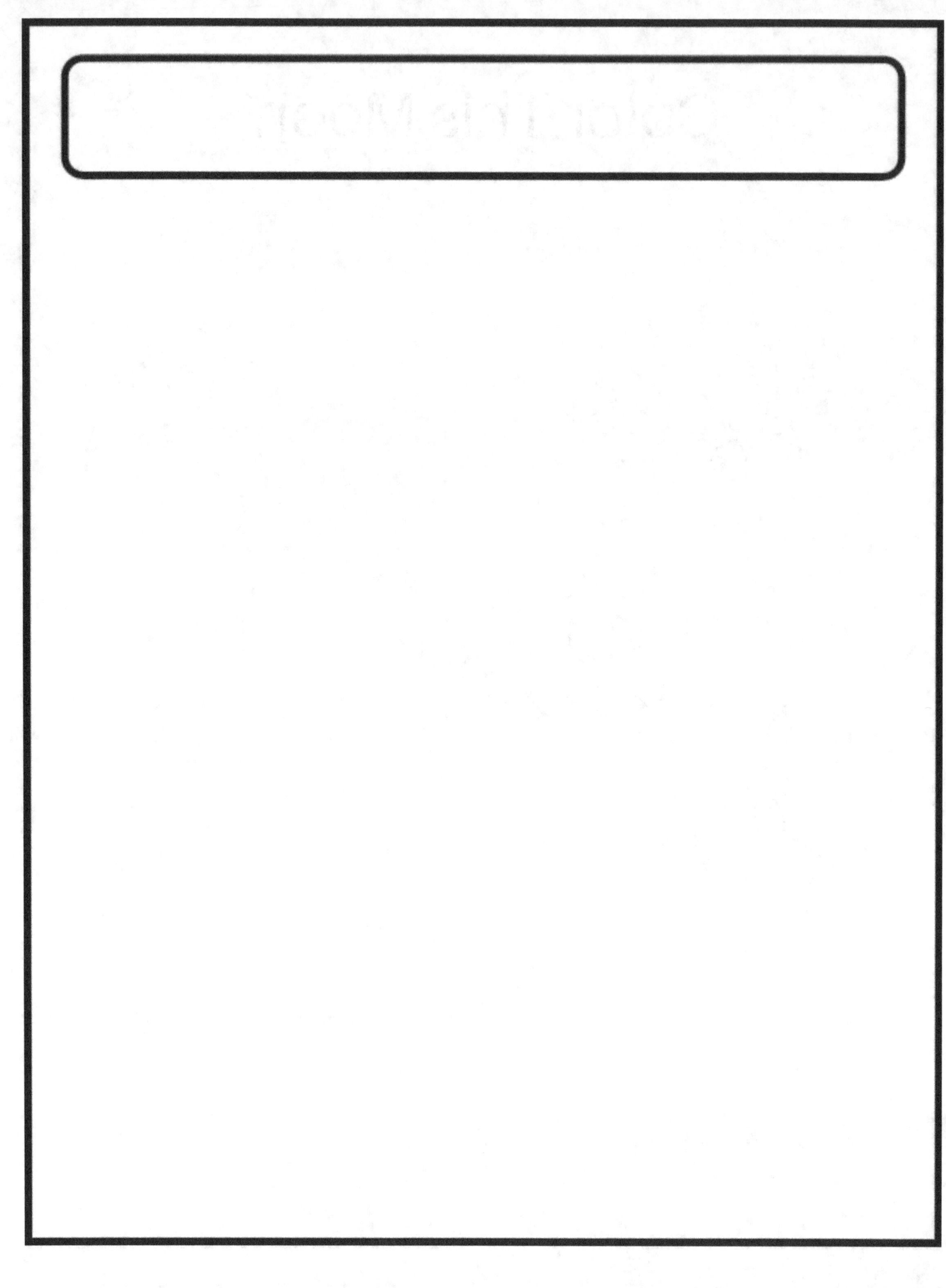

Color This Moon

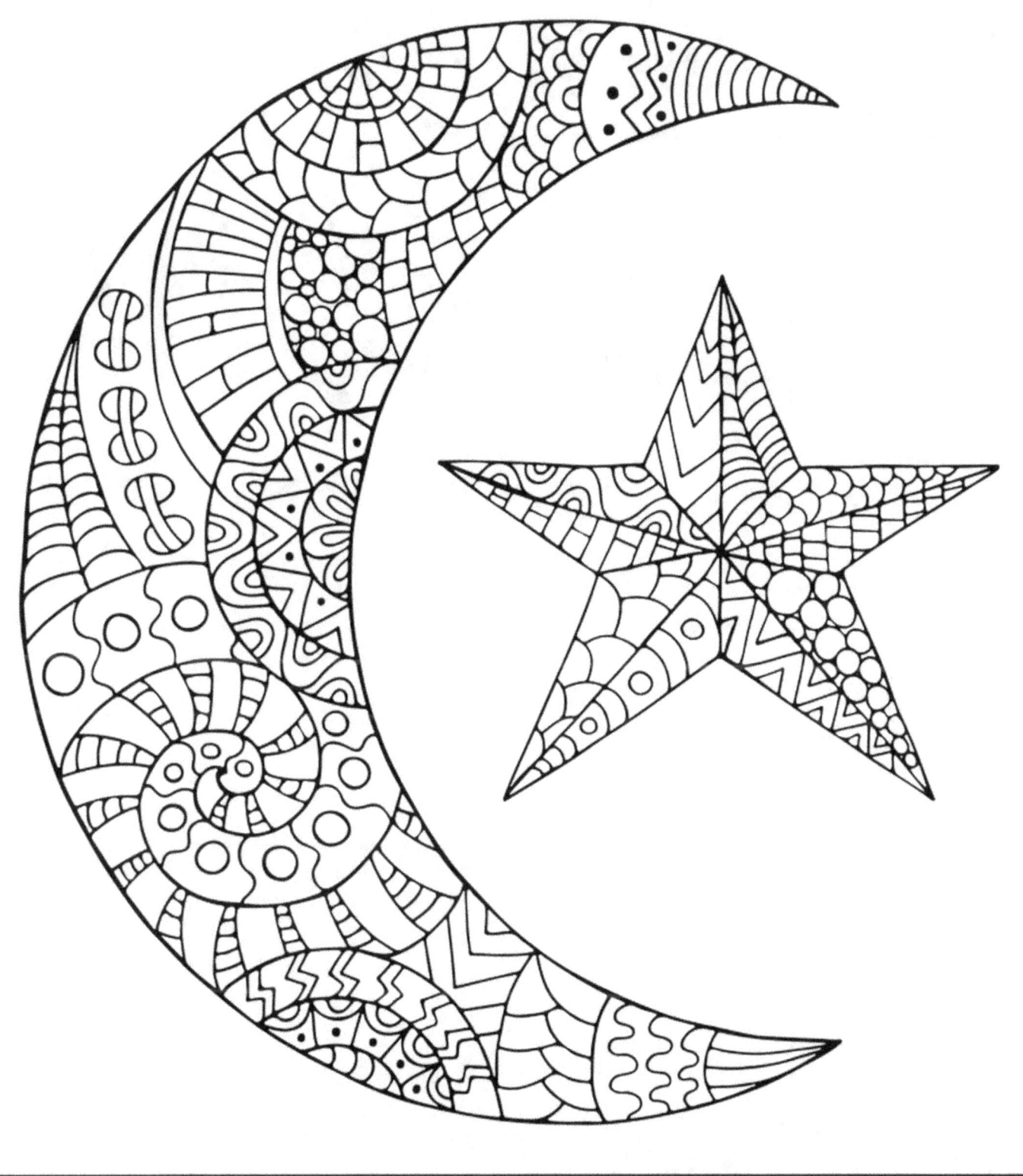

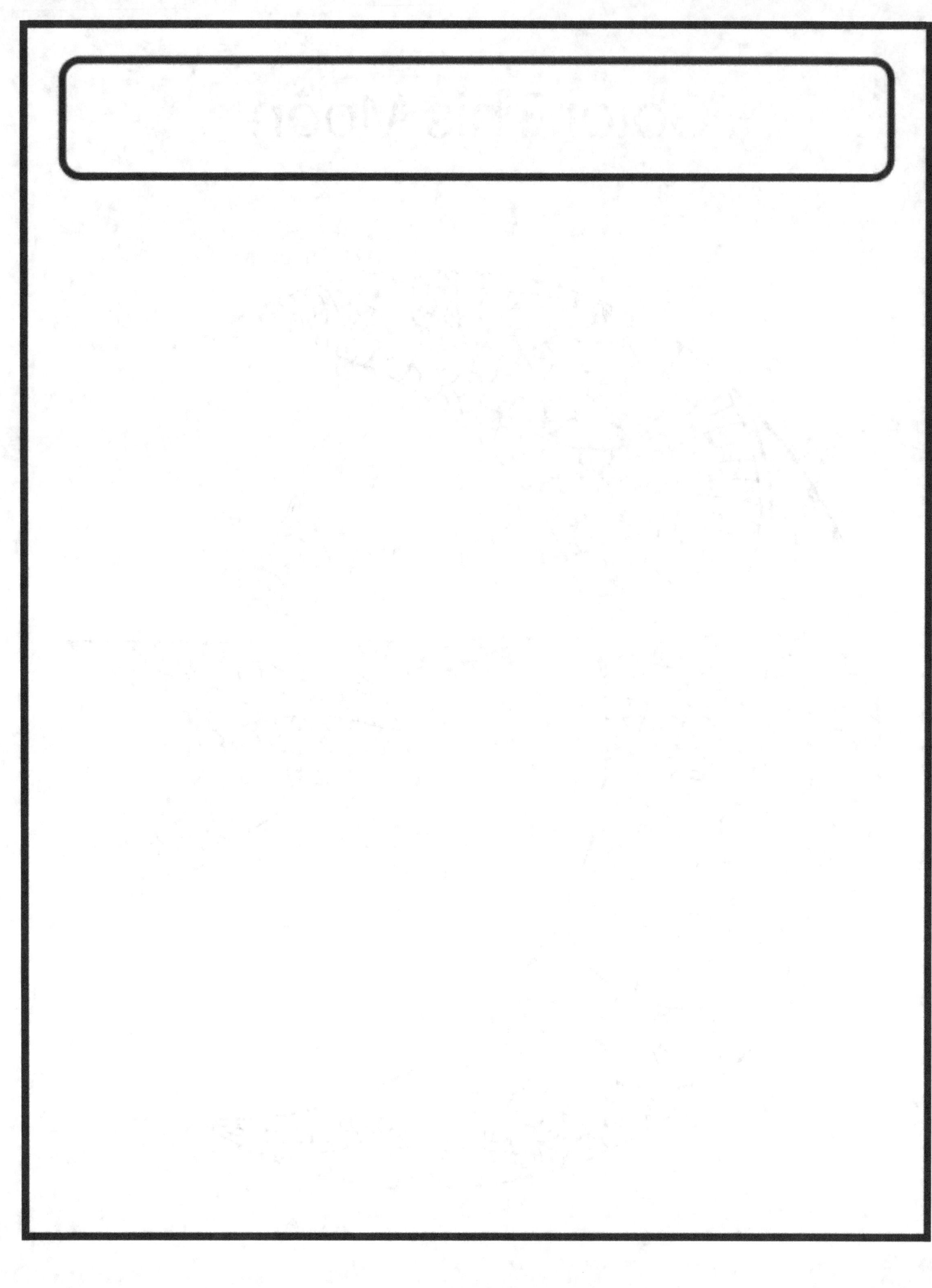

Color This Moon

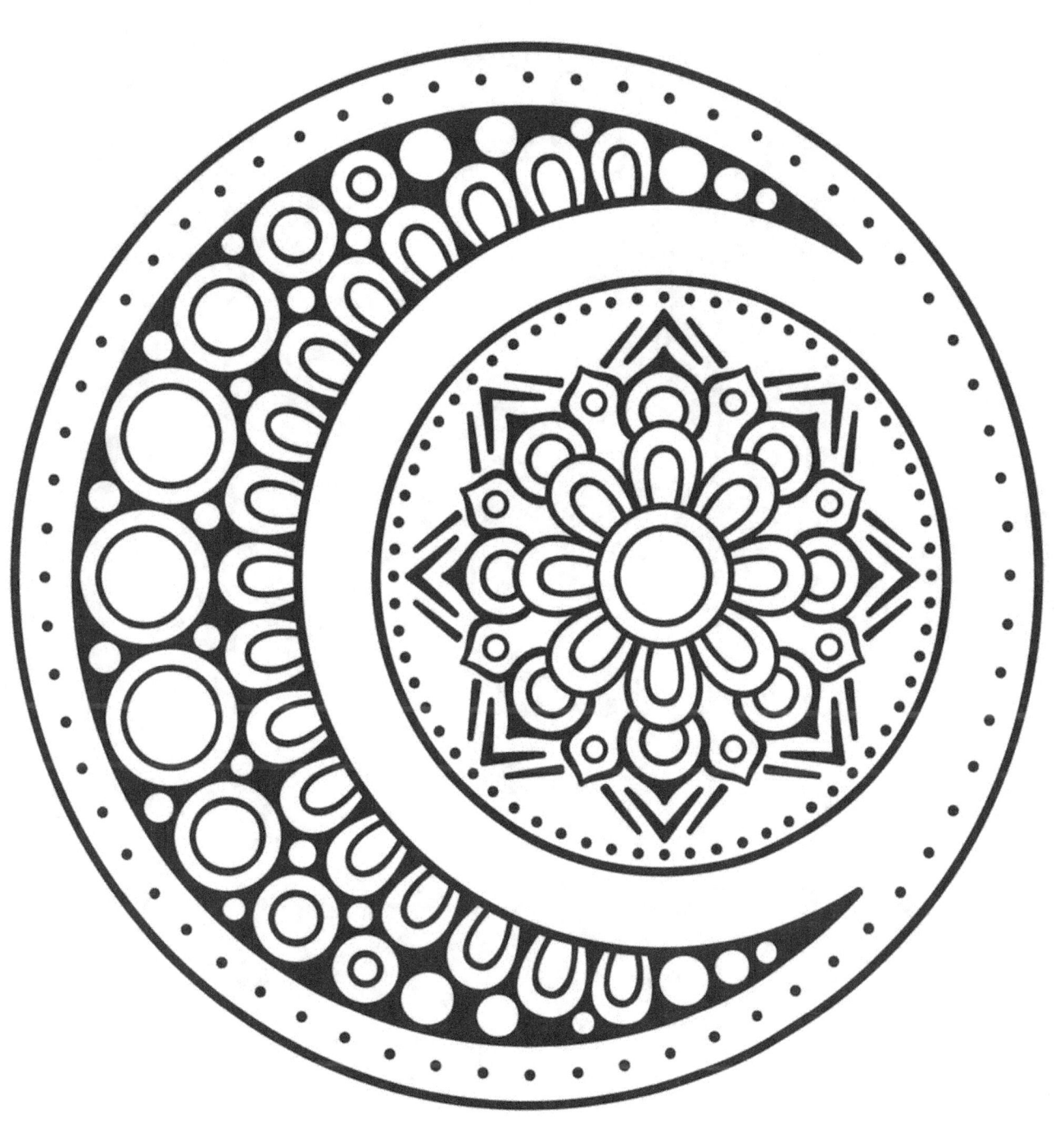

Color This Moon

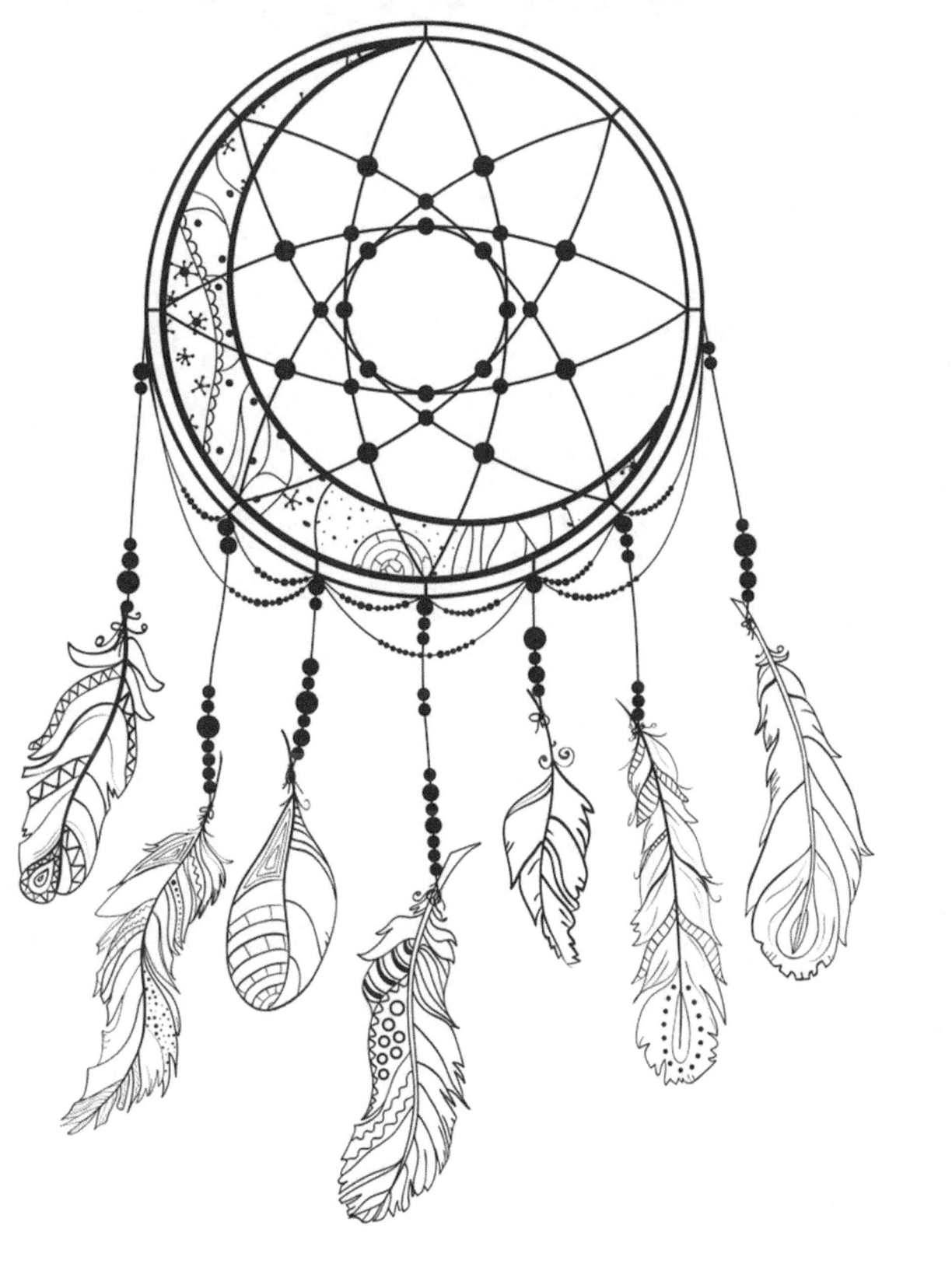

Color This Moon

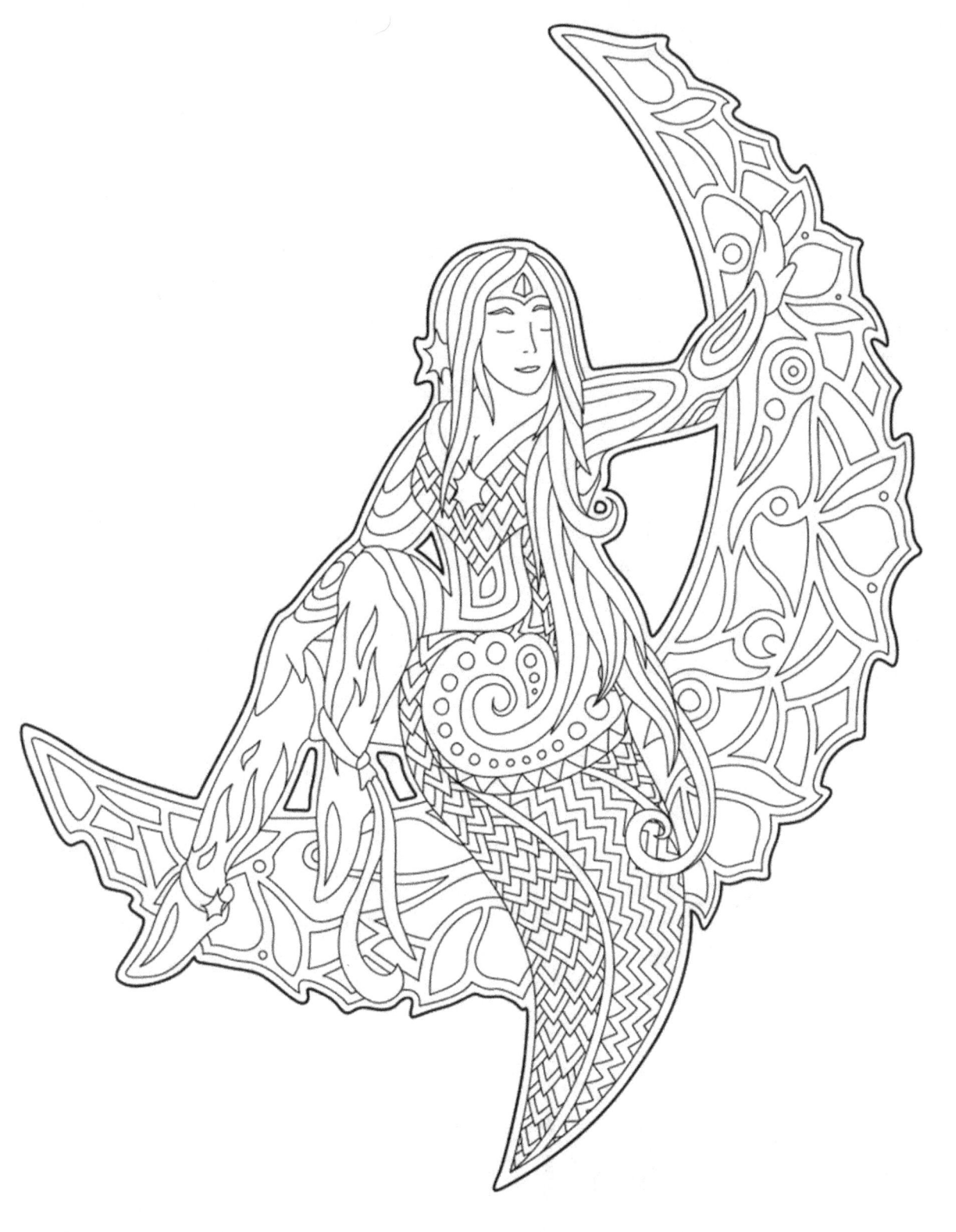

Color This Moon

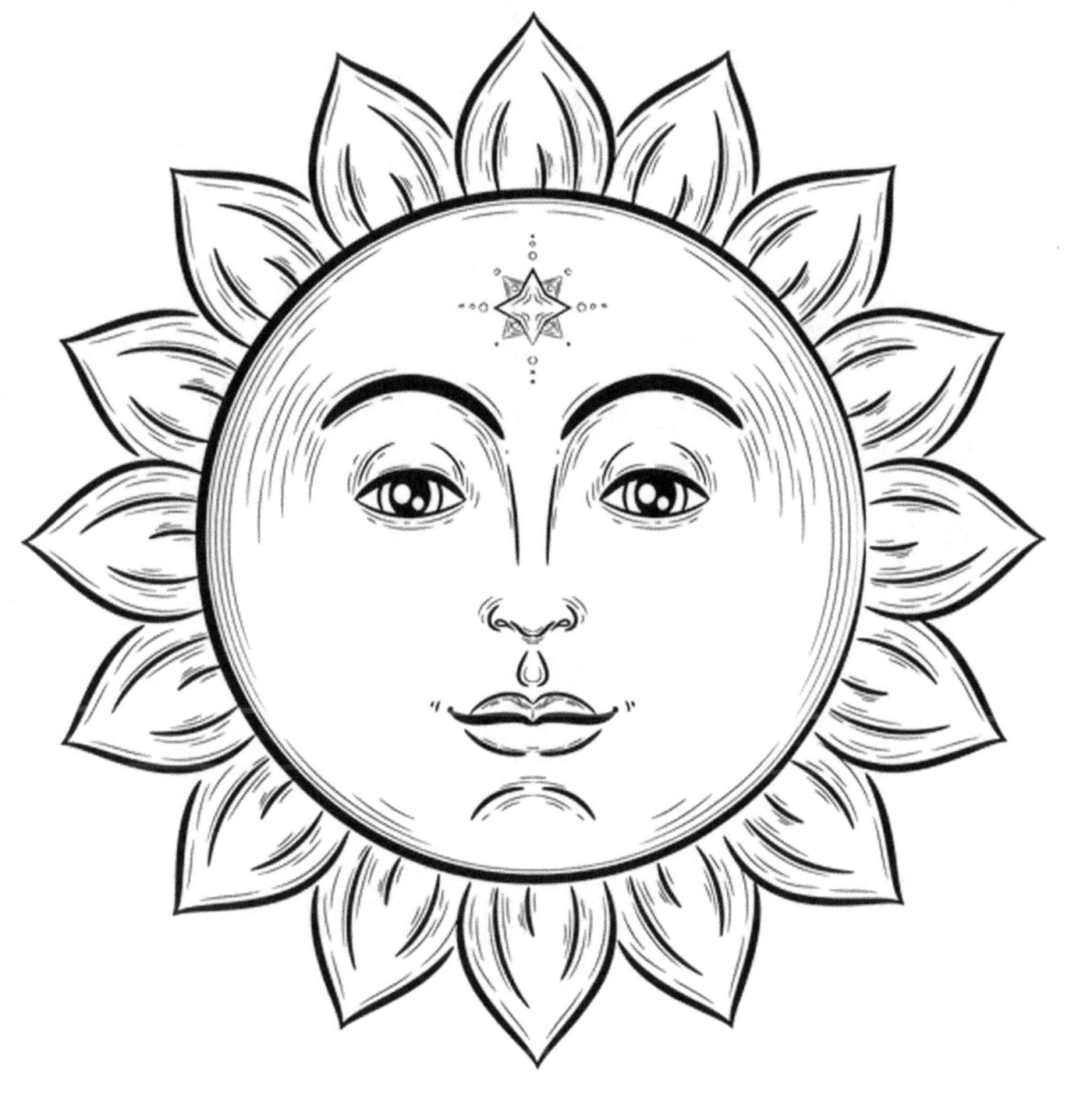

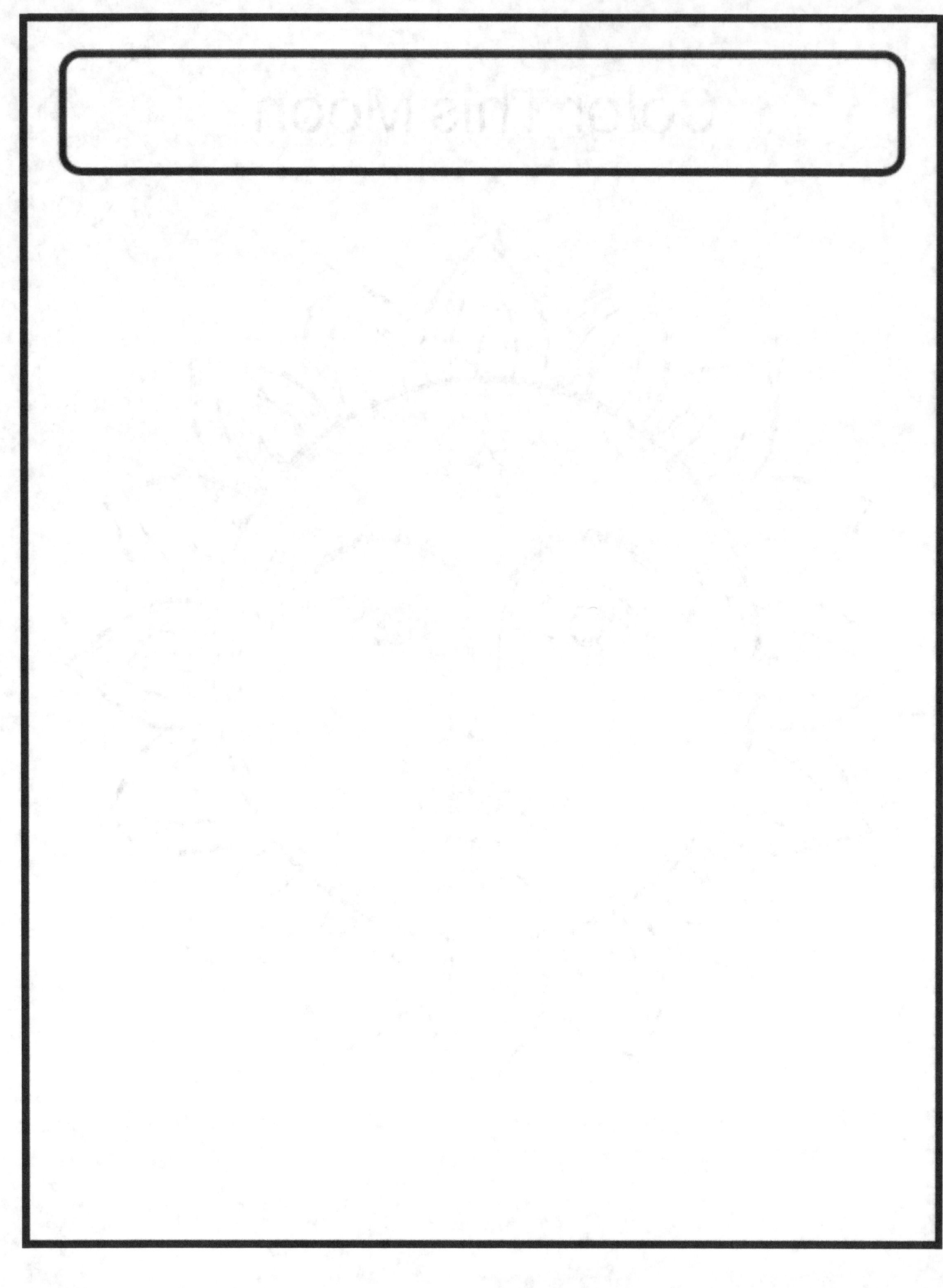

Color This Moon

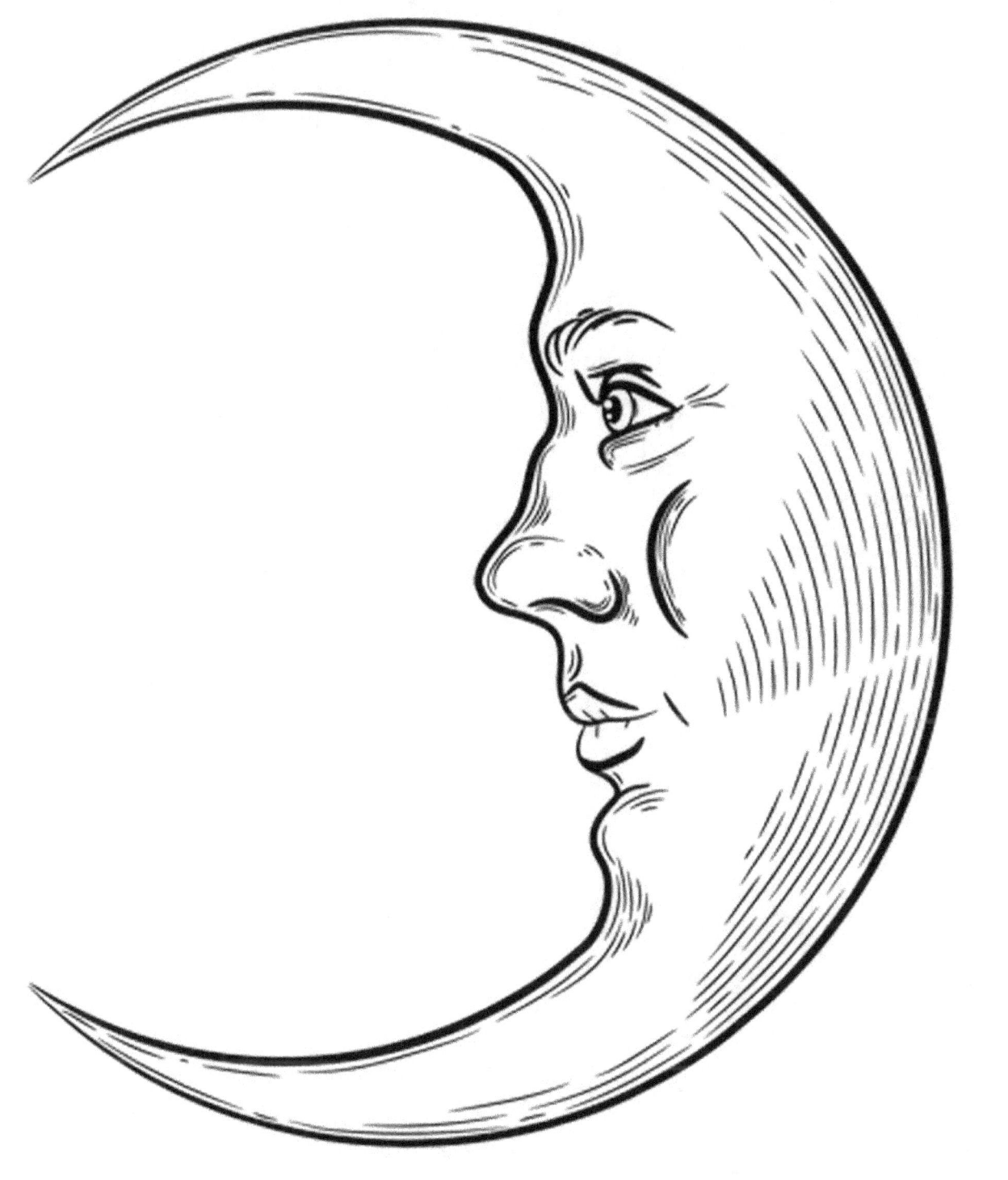

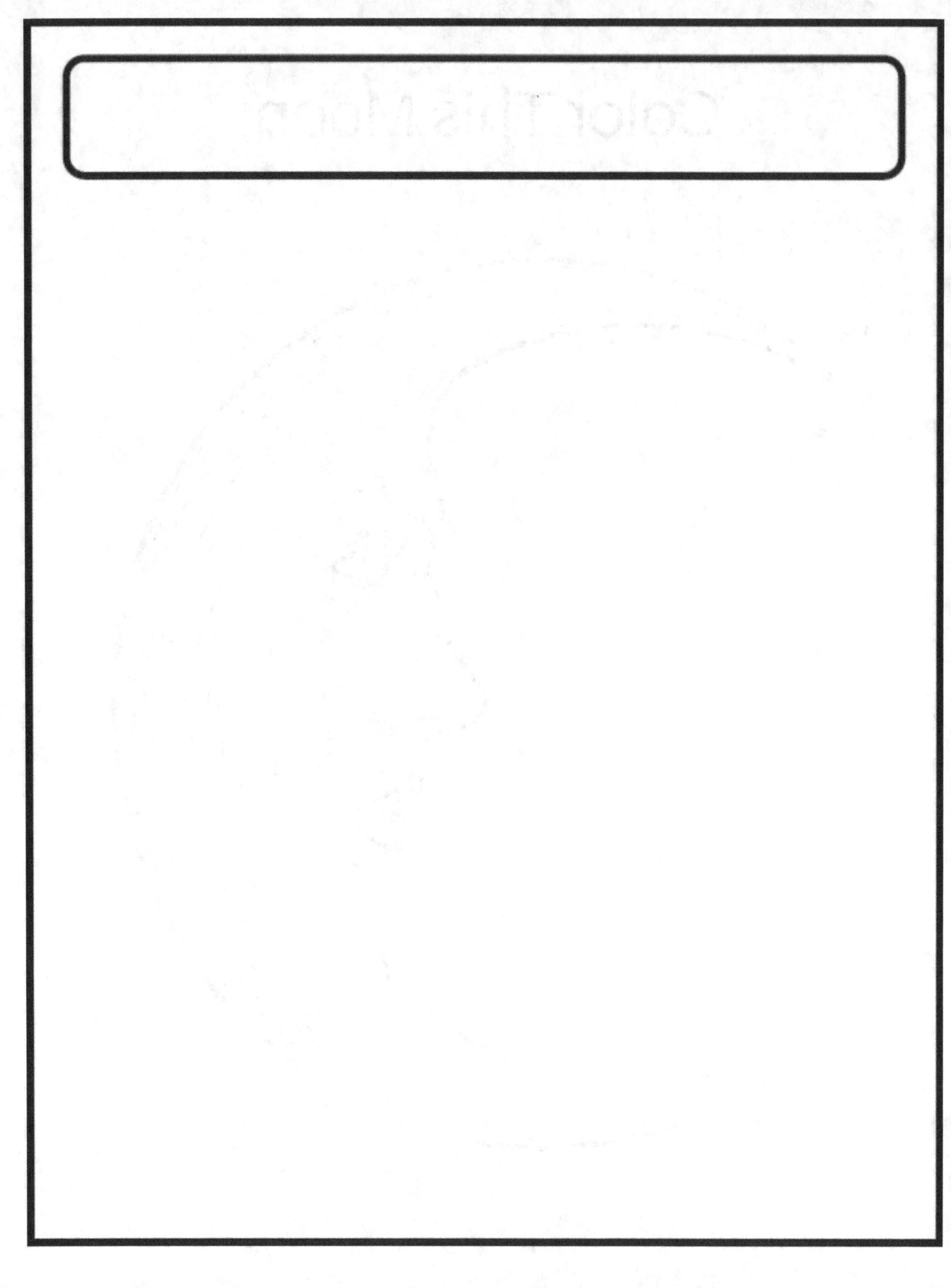

Color This Moon

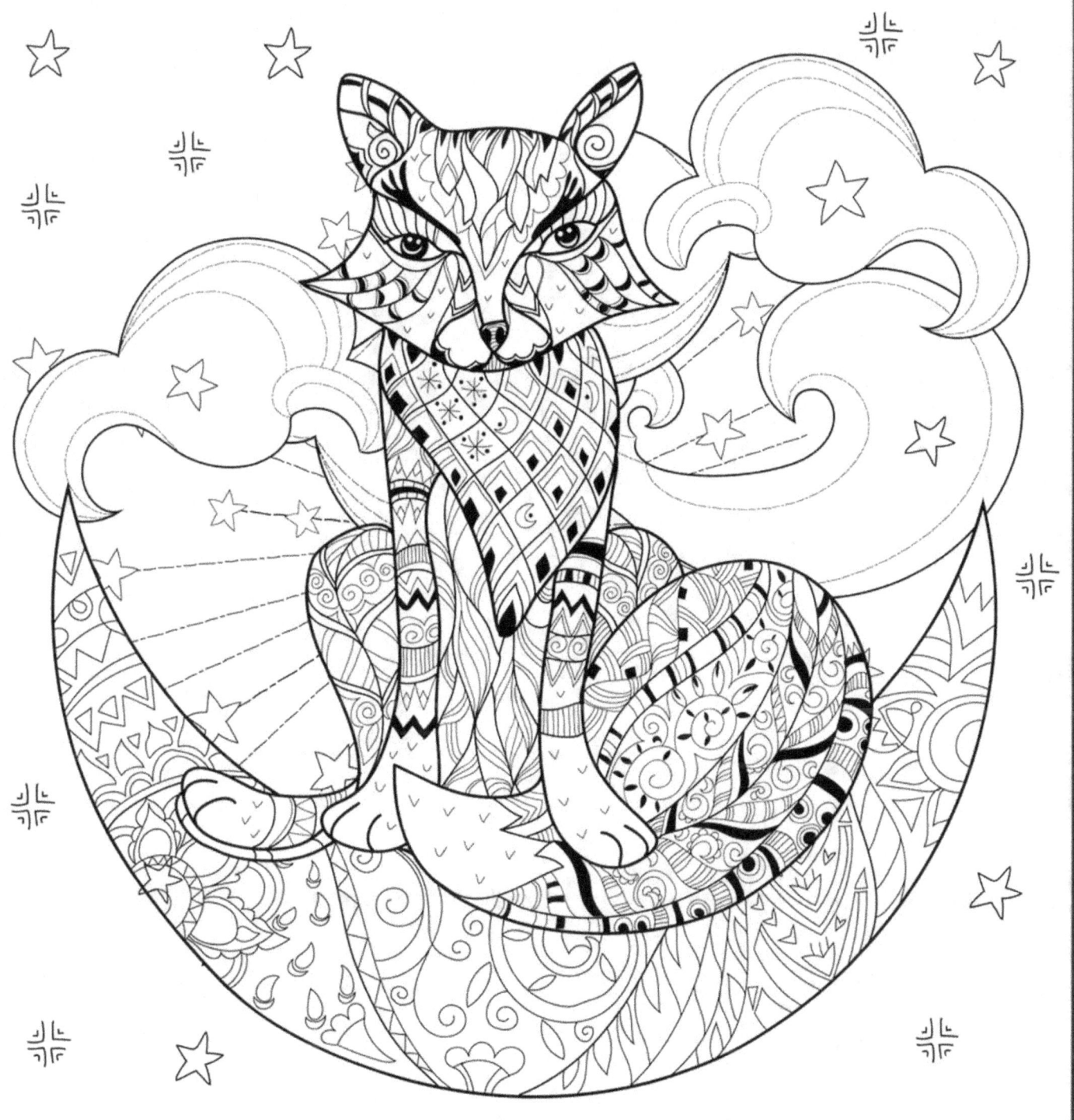

Color This Moon

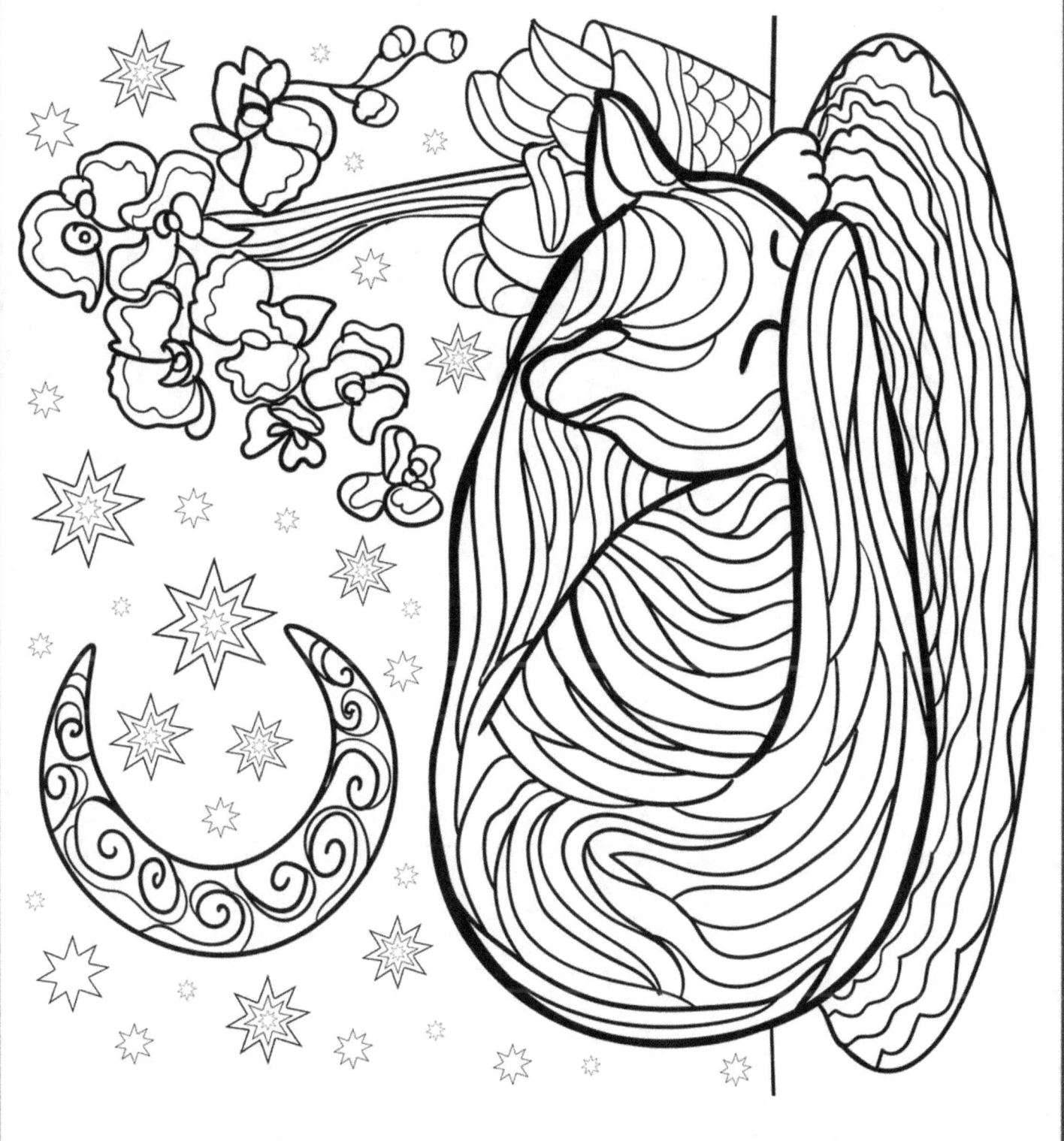

Color This Moon

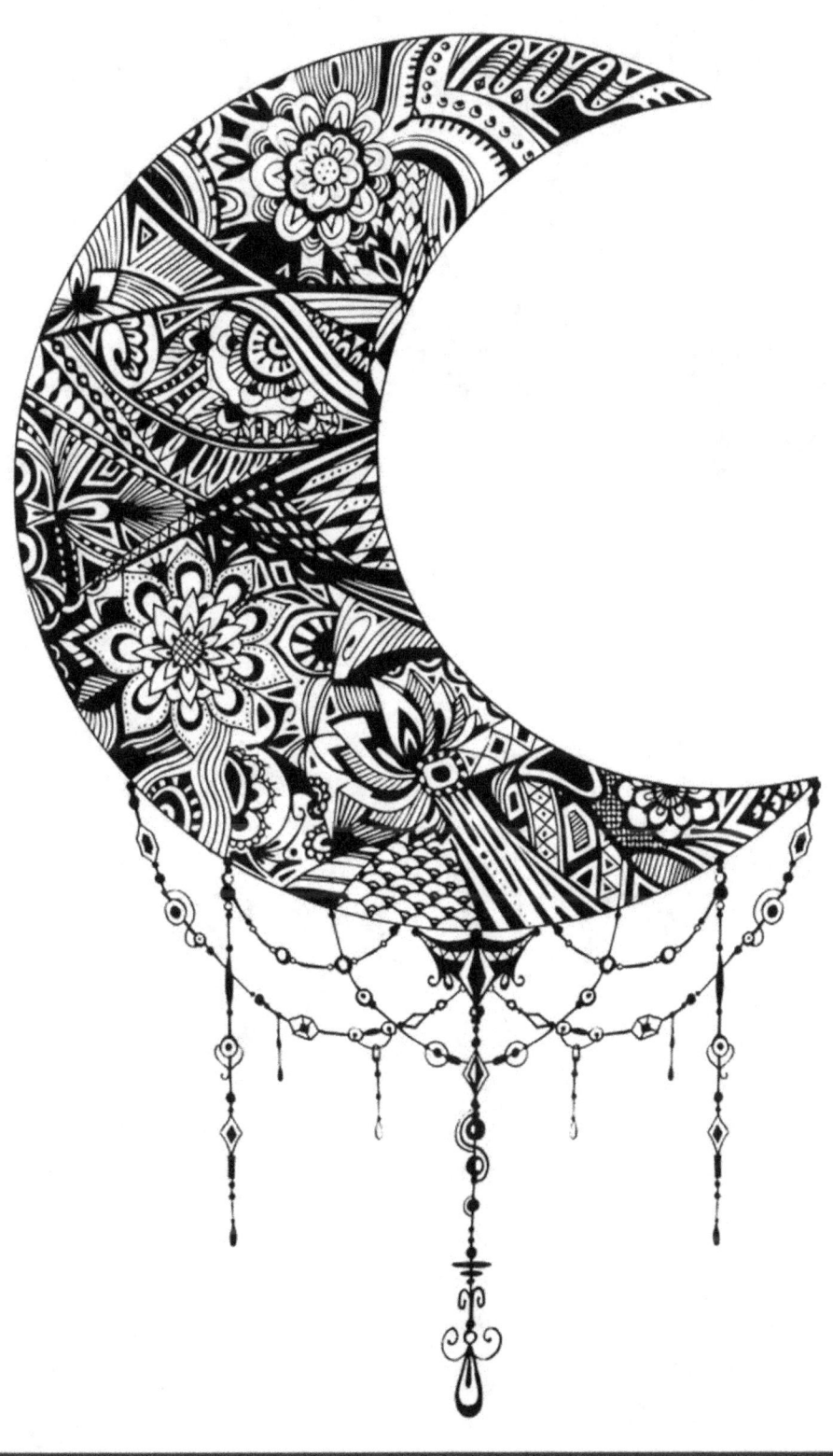

Color This Moon

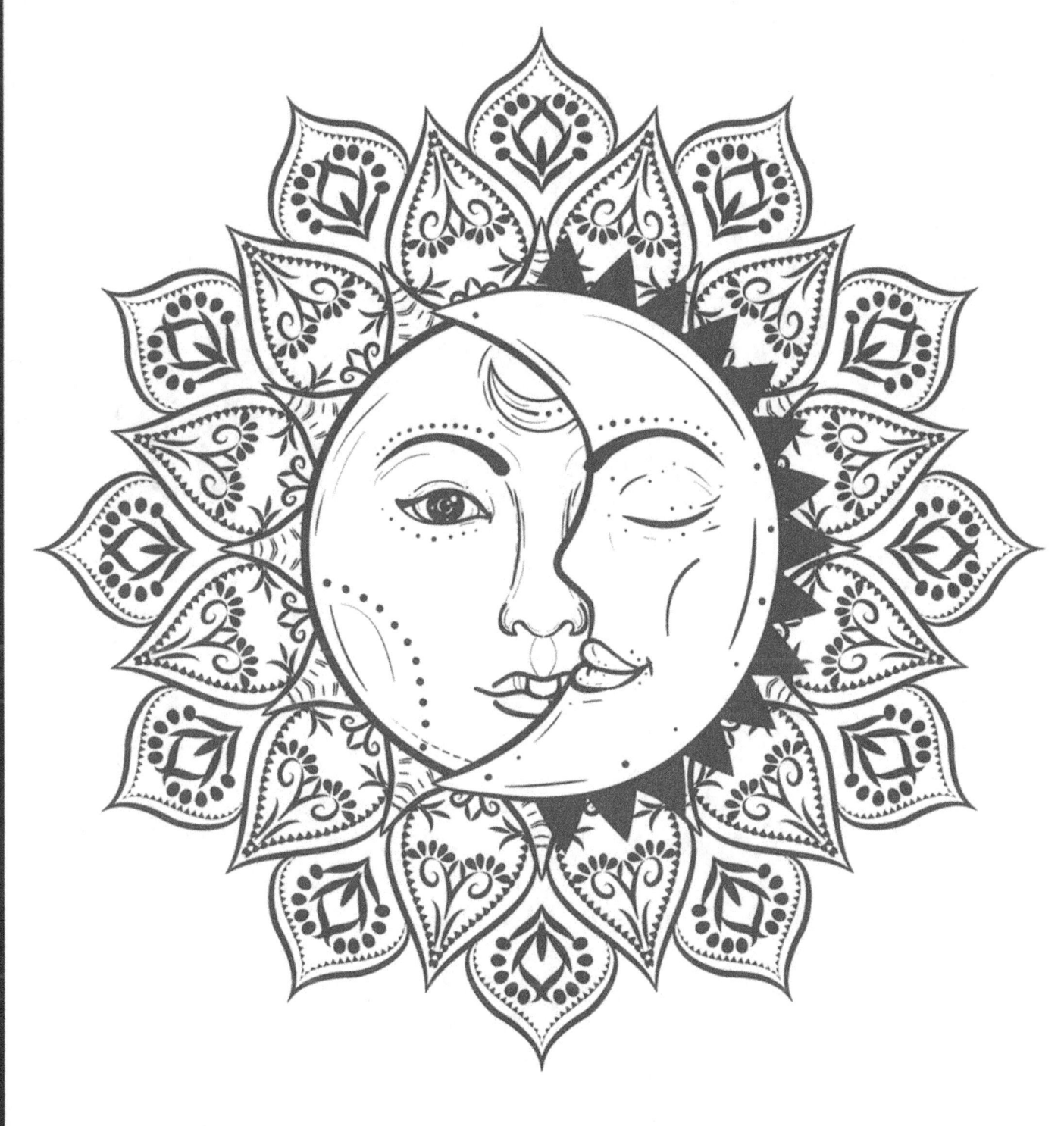

Color This Moon

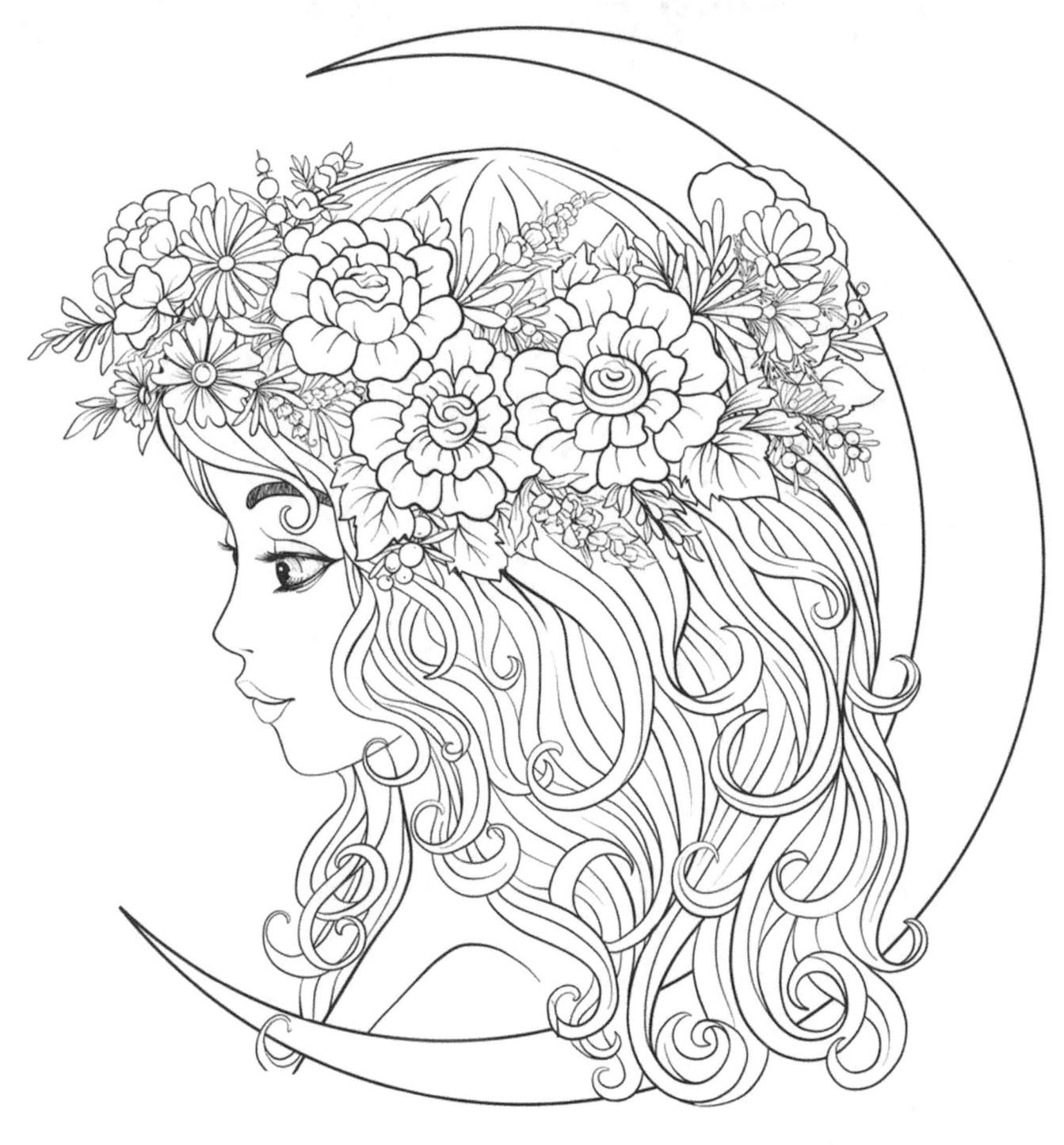

Color This Moon

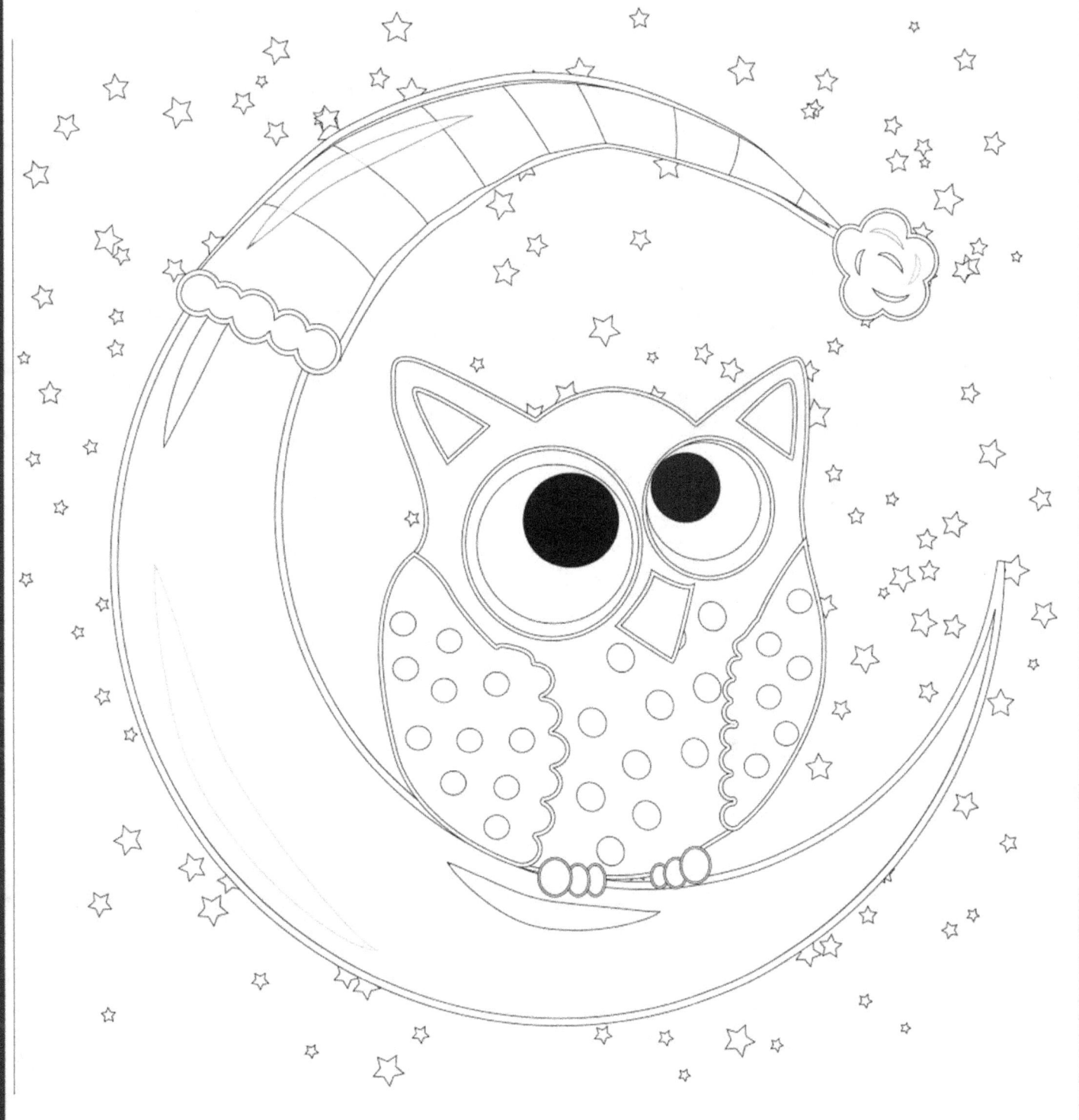

Color This Moon

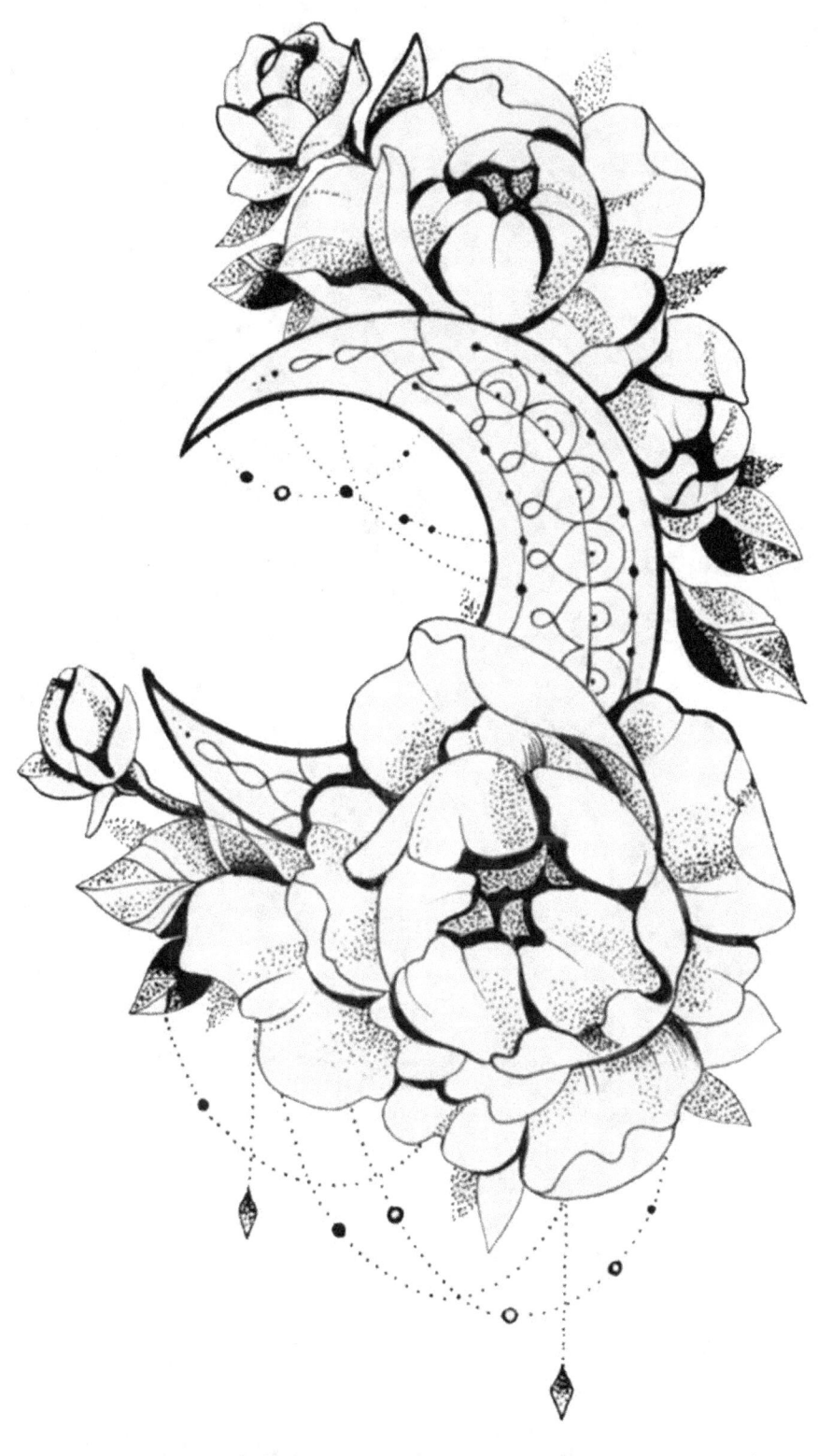

Color This Moon

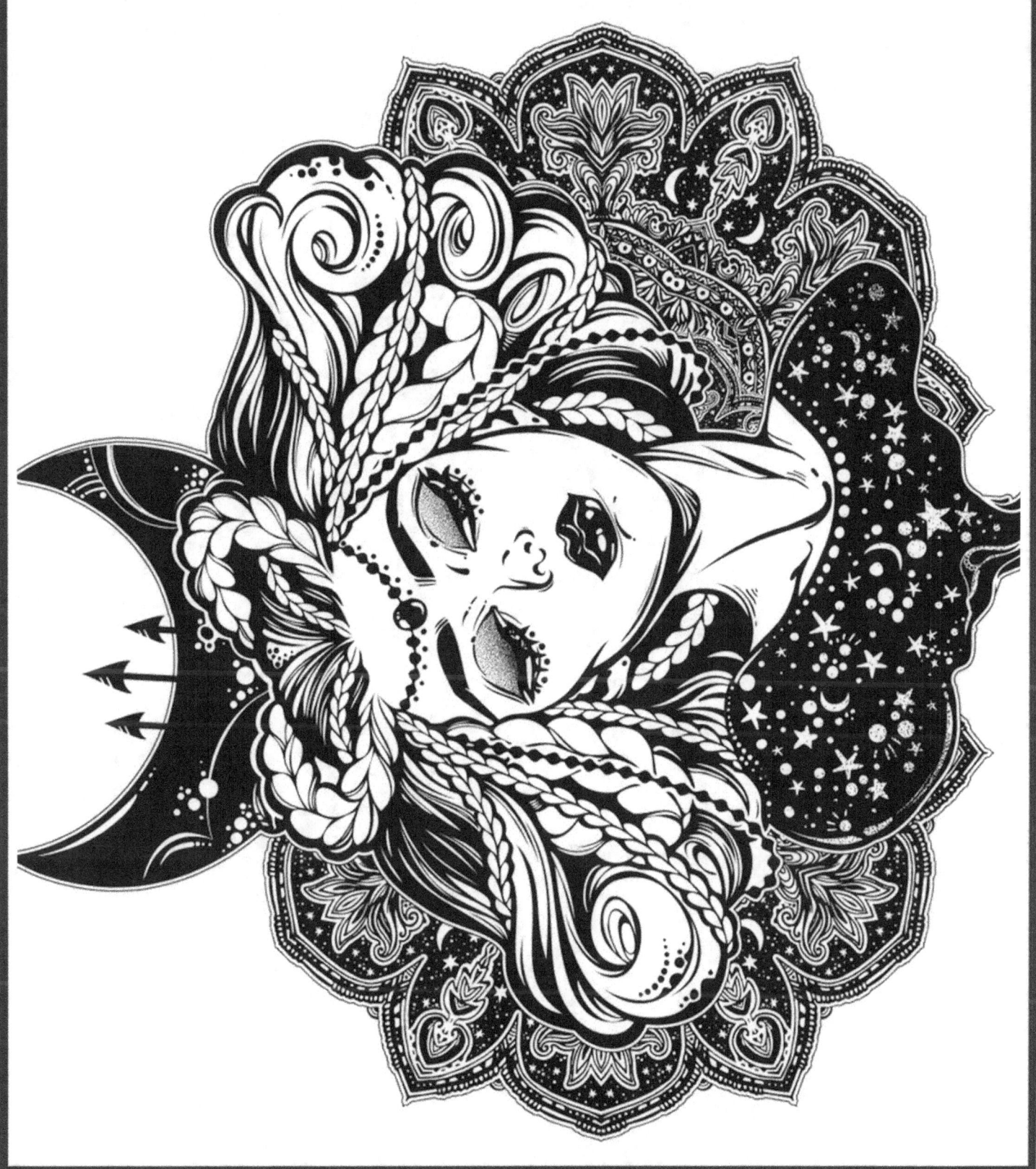

Color This Moon

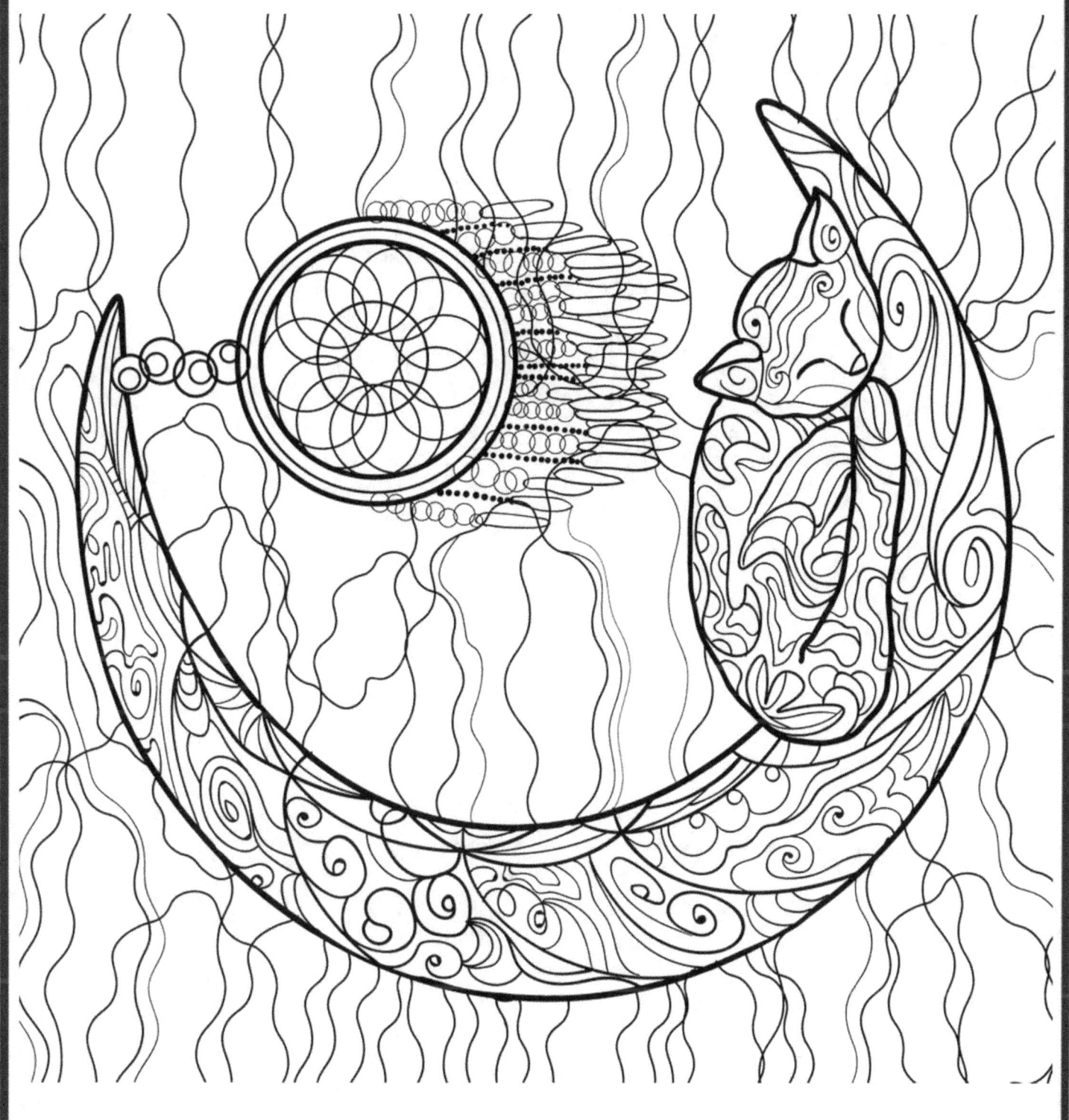

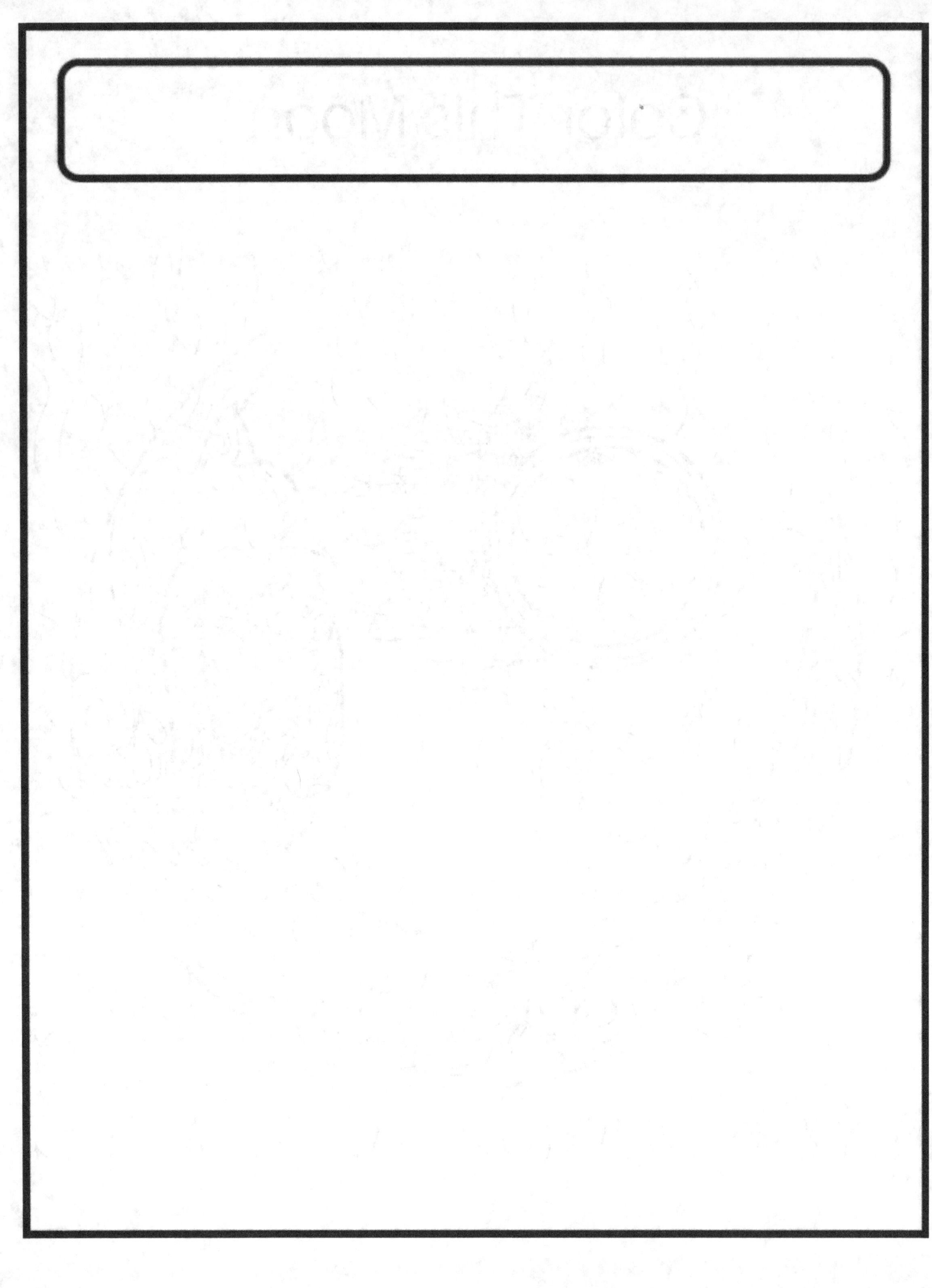

Color This Moon

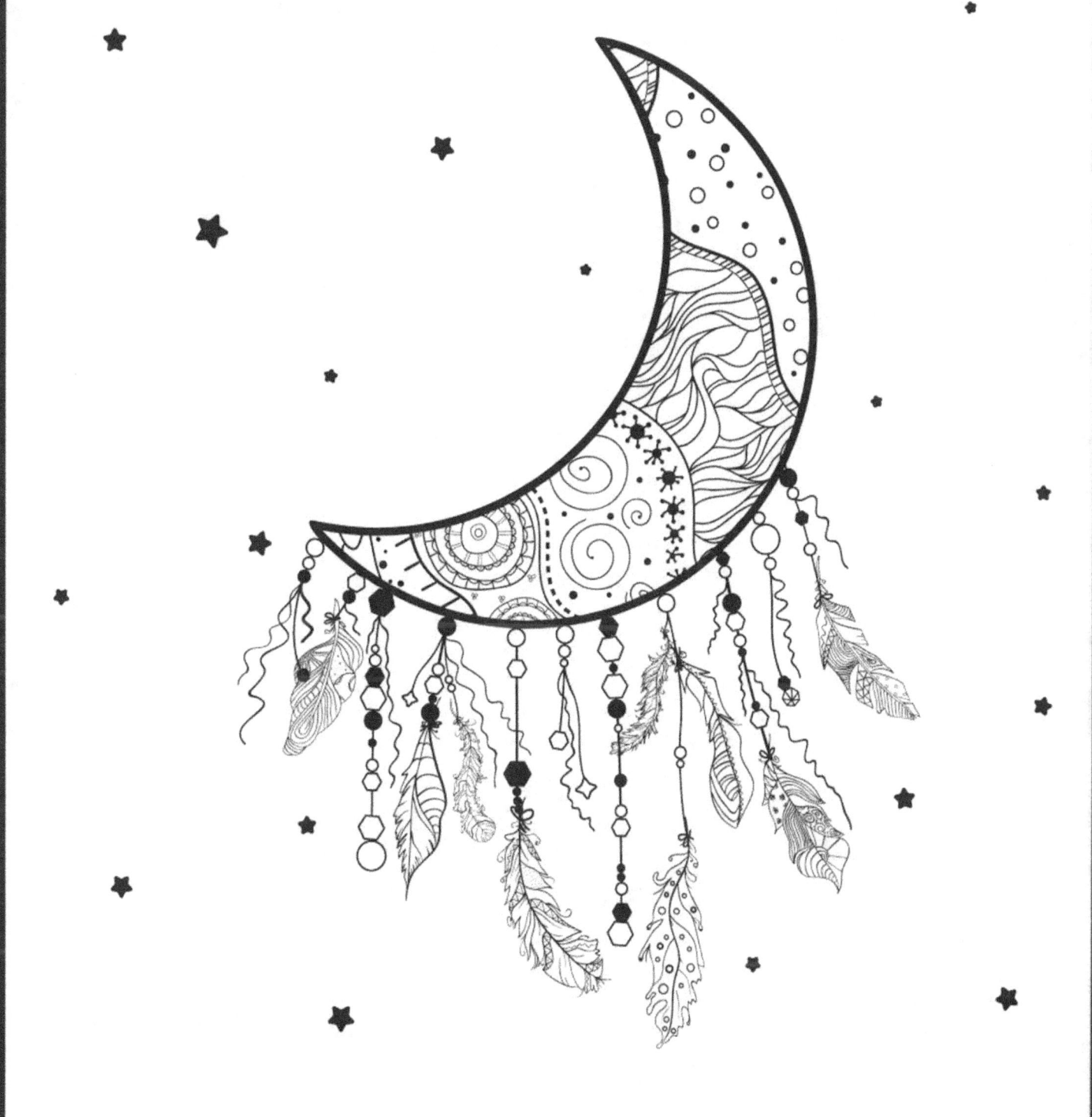

Color This Moon

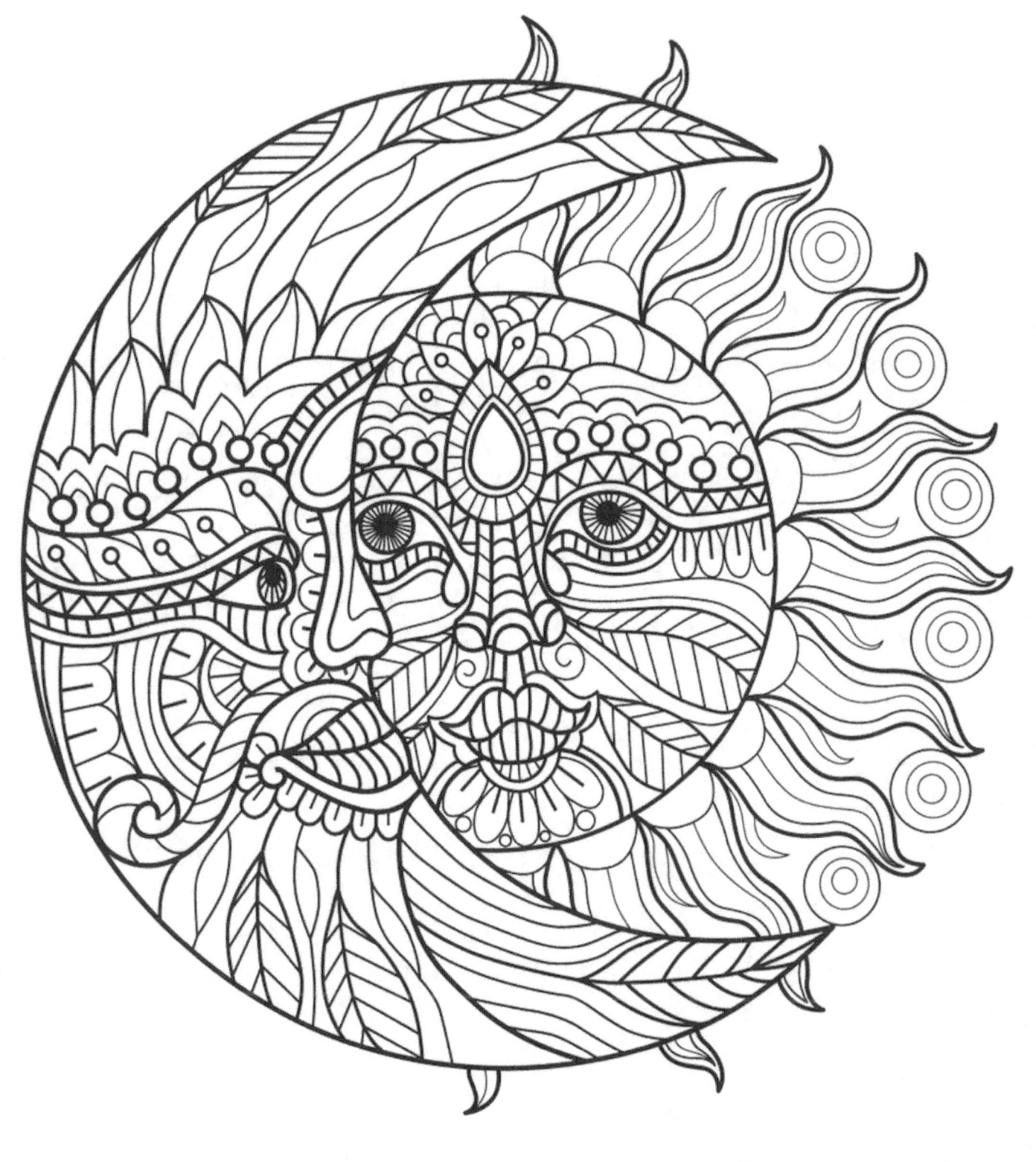

Color This Moon

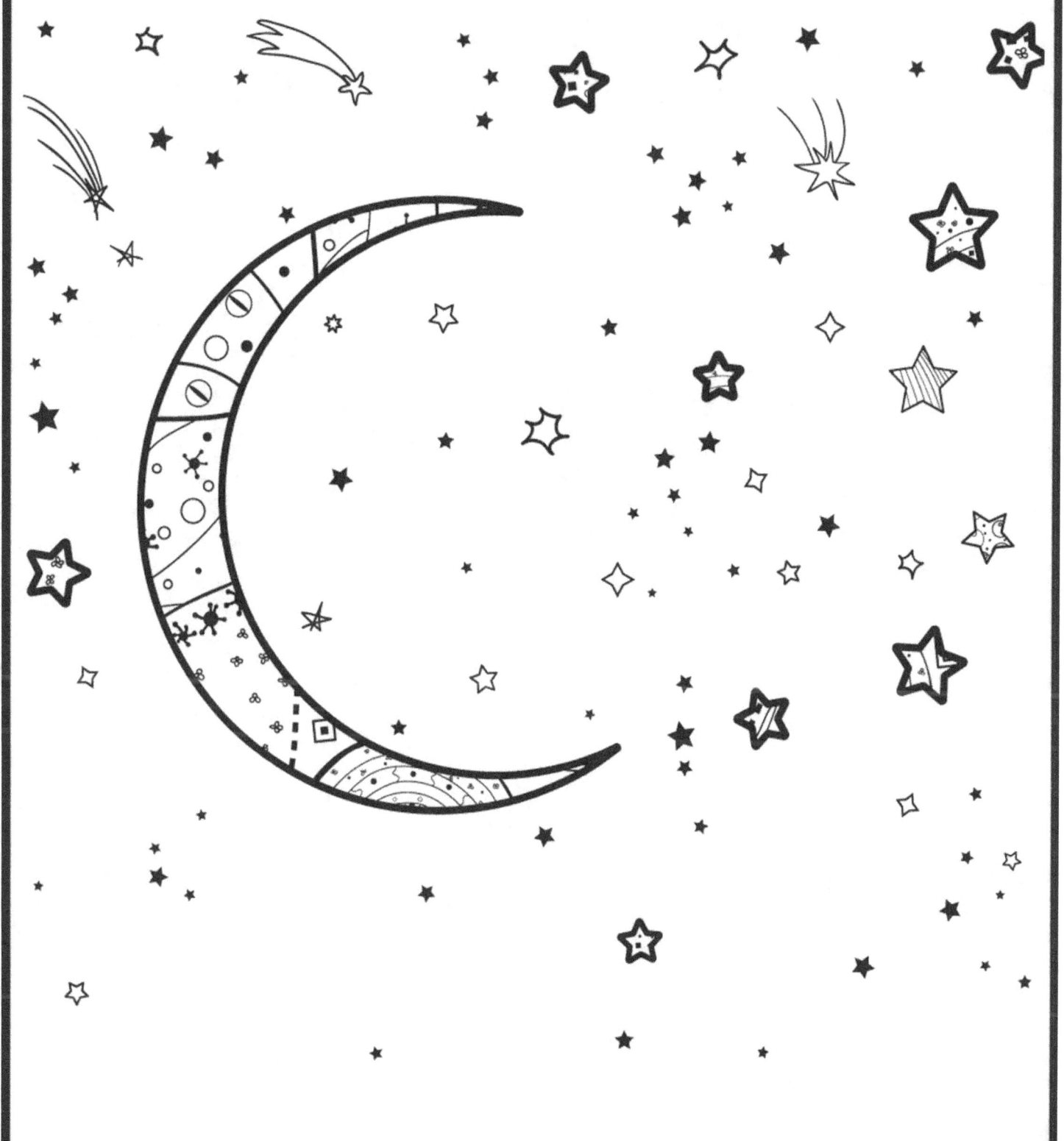

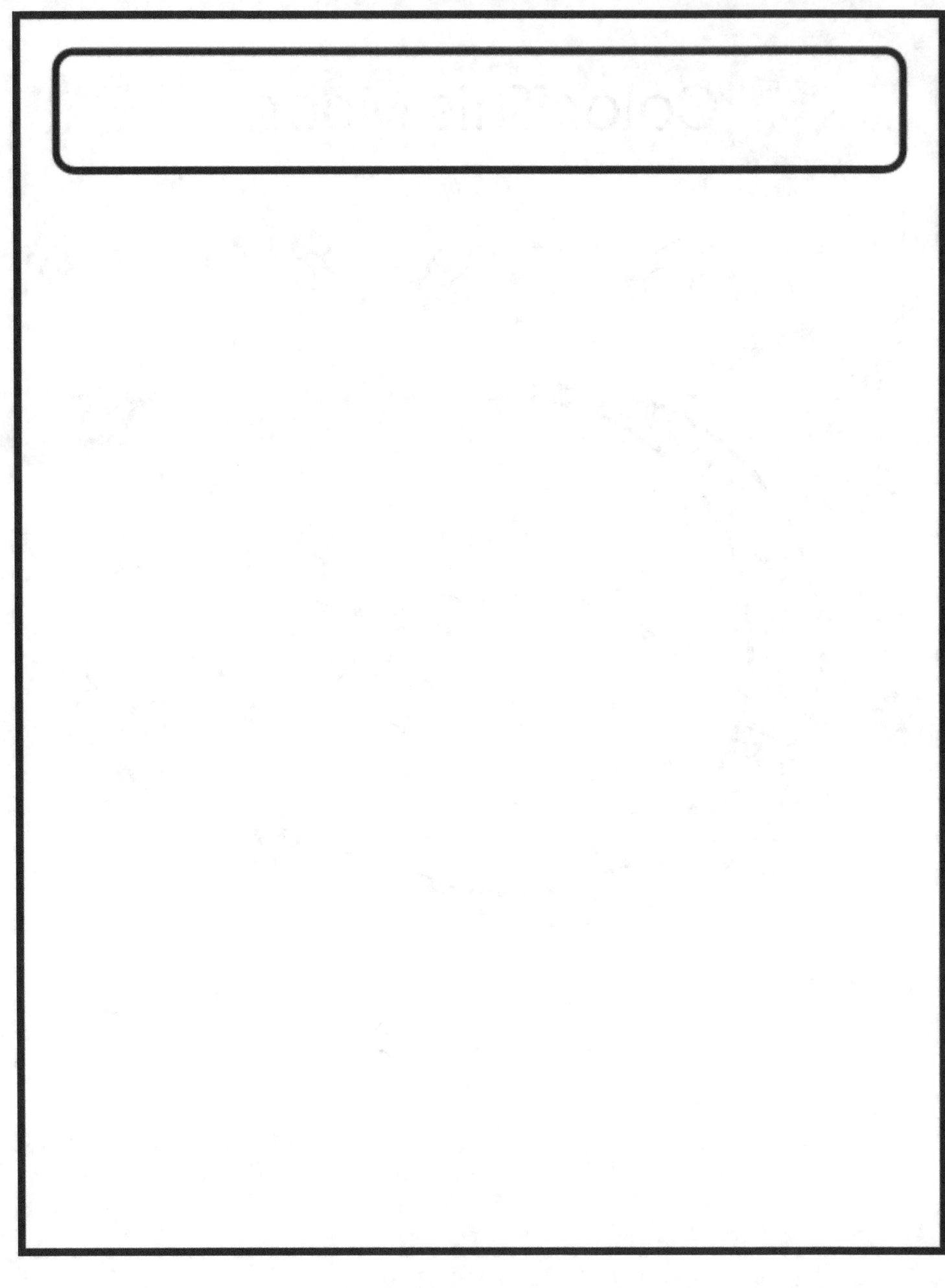

Color This Moon

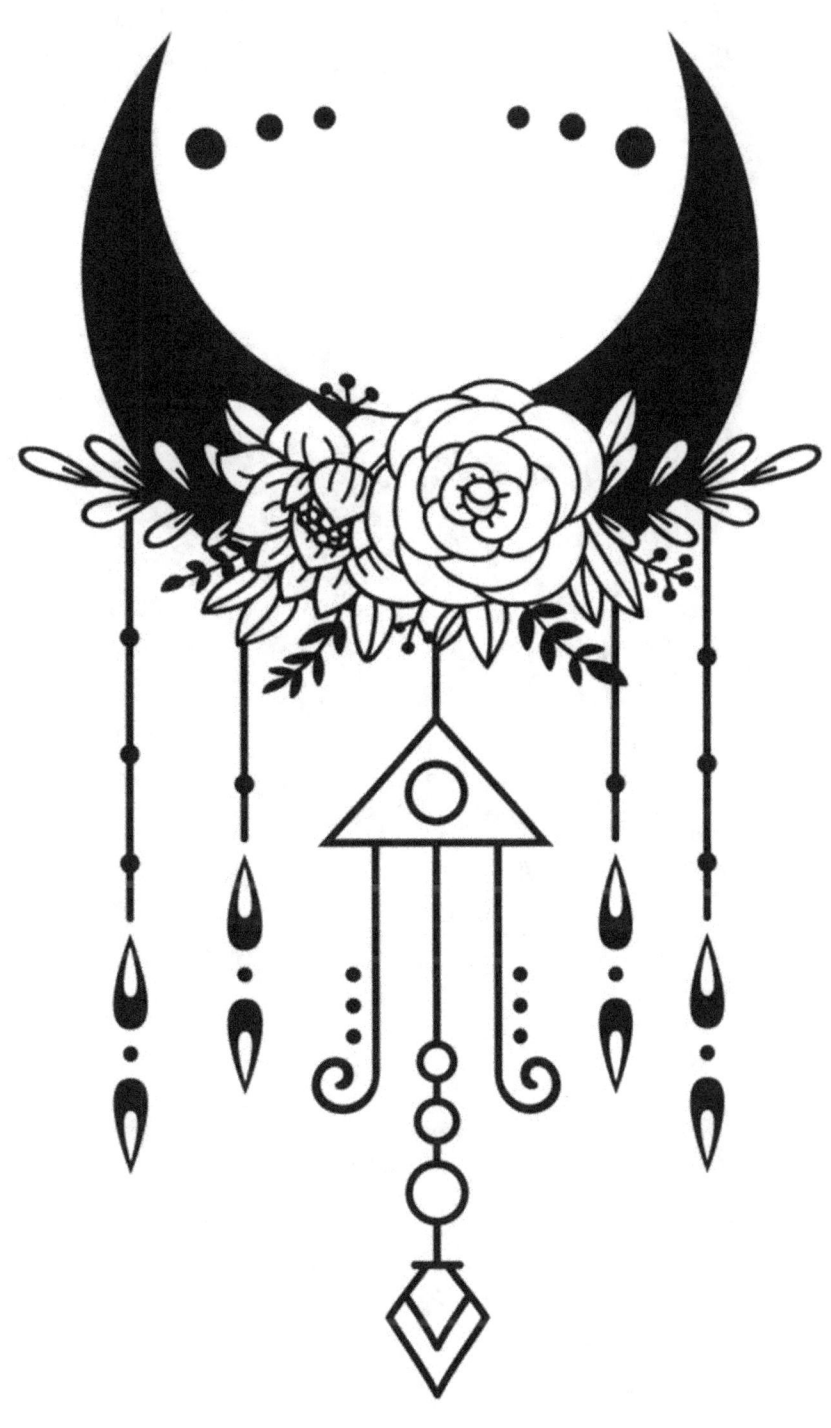

Color This Moon

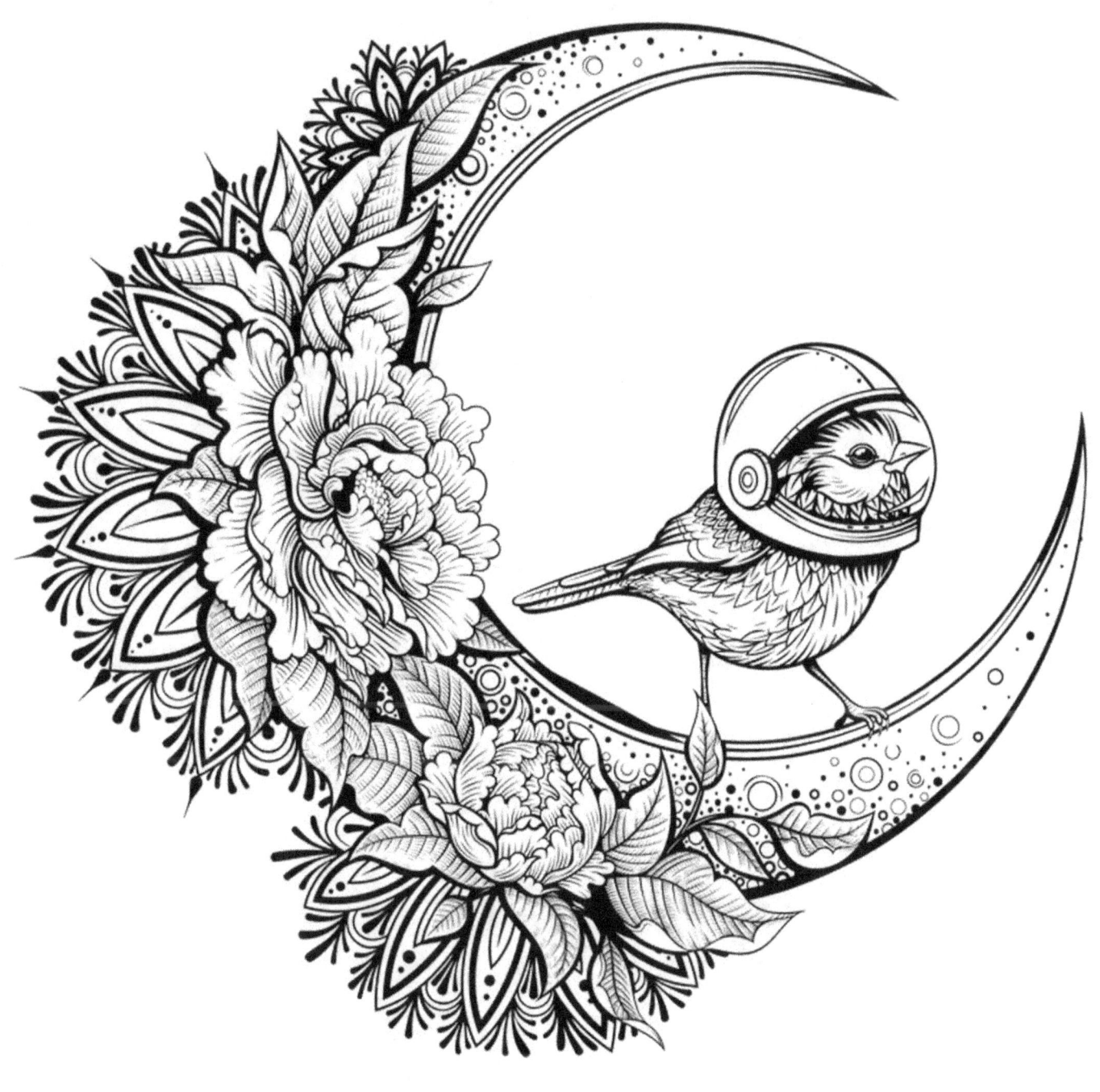

Color This Moon

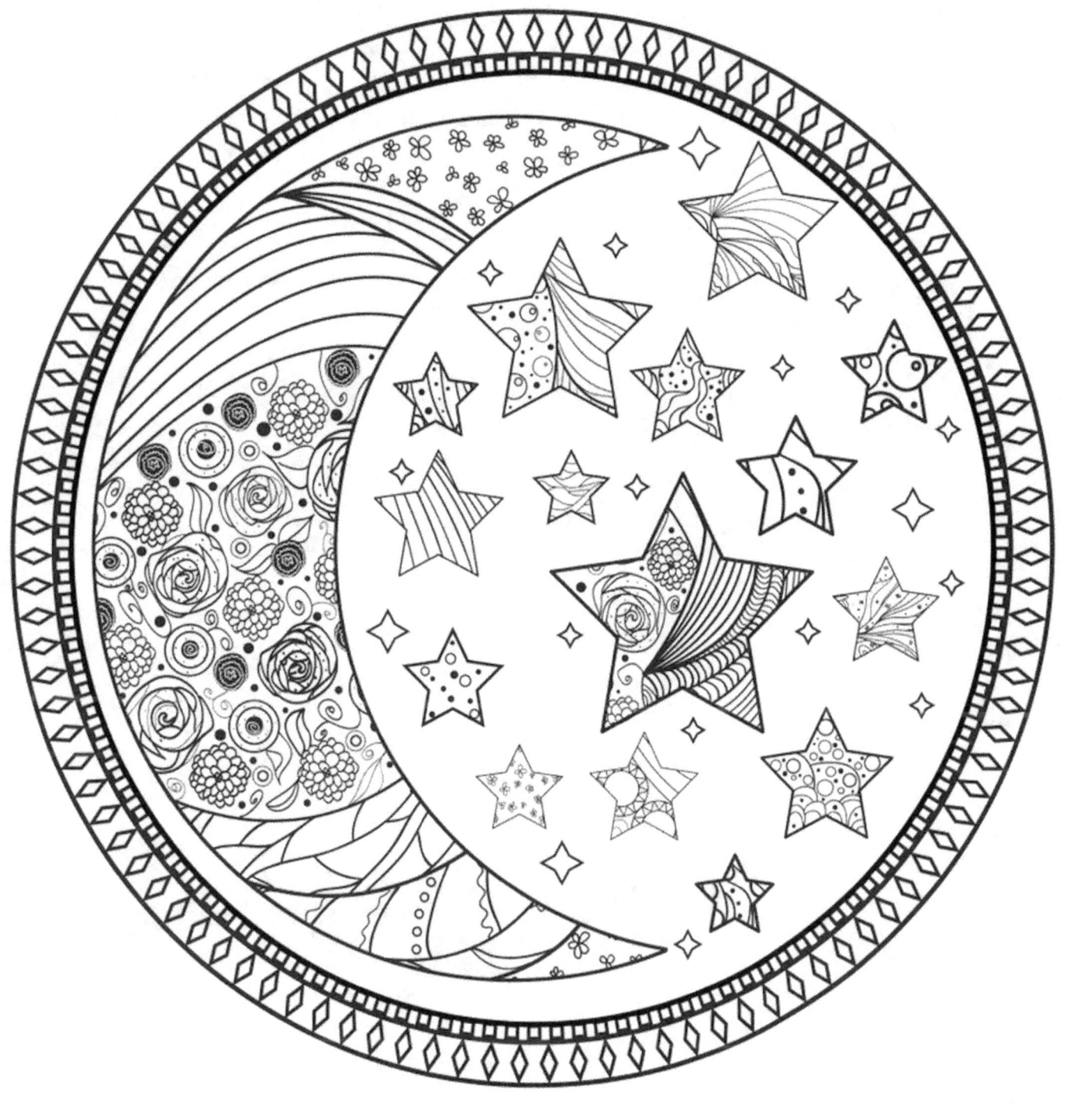

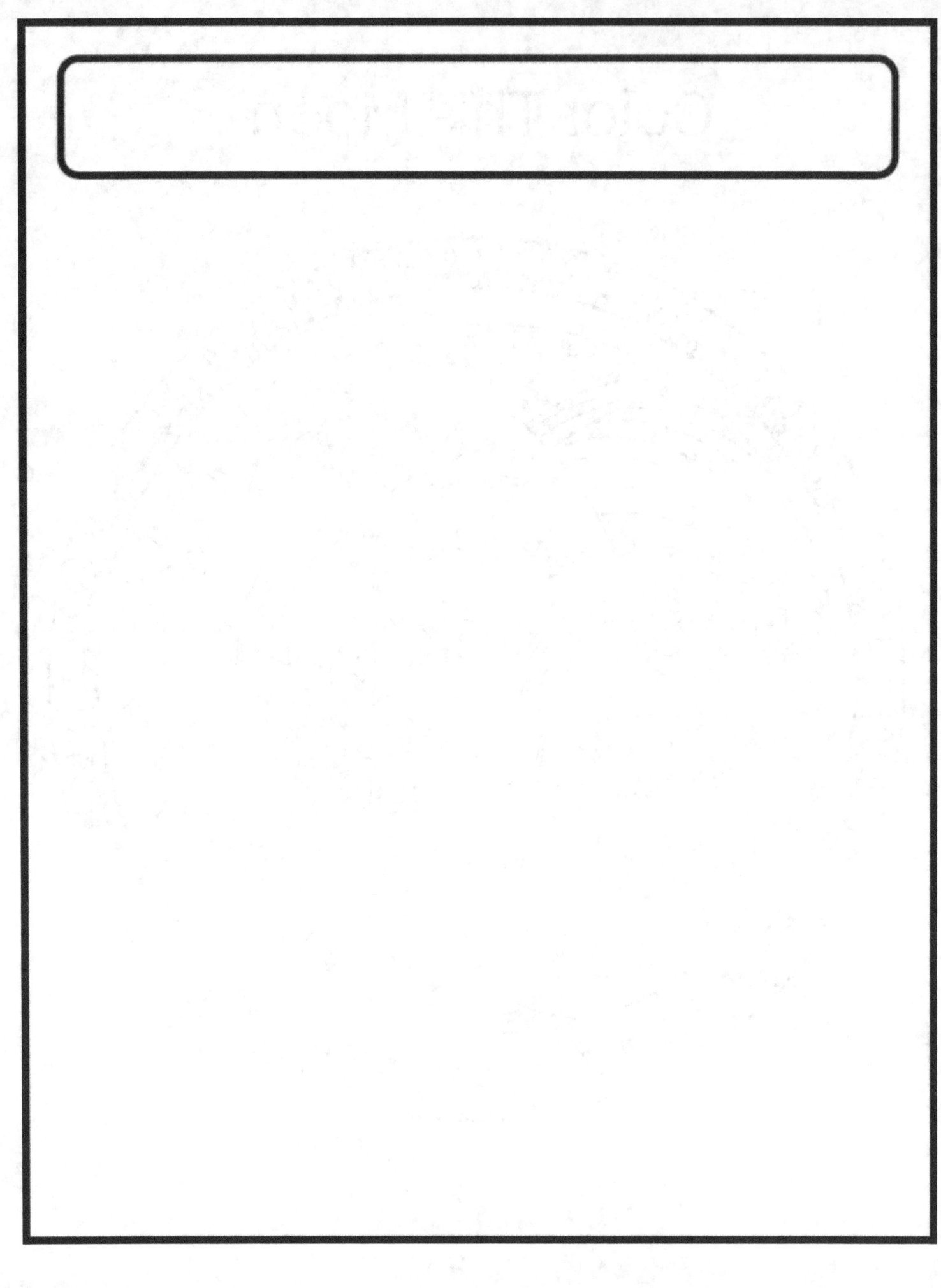

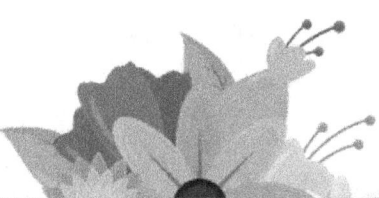

Scan This Qr Code And Visit Our
Author Page At-
amazon.com

www.ingramcontent.com/pod-product-compliance
Lightning Source LLC
Chambersburg PA
CBHW080529220526
45465CB00006B/2652